VICTORIAN LITERATURE SIXTY YEARS OF BOOKS AND BOOKMEN BY CLEMENT SHORTER

BURT FRANKLIN
NEW YORK

Published by LENOX HILL Pub. & Dist. Co. (Burt Franklin)
235 East 44th St., New York, N.Y. 10017
Originally Published: 1897
Reprinted: 1970
Printed in the U.S.A.

S.B.N.: 8337-32579
Library of Congress Card Catalog No.: 78-143658
Burt Franklin: Bibliography & Reference 385

Reprinted from the original edition in the University of
Illinois Libraries.

INTRODUCTORY

ASKED by a kindly publisher to add one more
to the Jubilee volumes which commemorate the
sixtieth year of the Queen's reign, I am pleased
at the opportunity thus afforded me of gather-
ing up a few impressions of pleasant reading
hours. "Every age," says Emerson, "must write
its own books ; or rather, each generation for the
next succeeding. The books of an older period
will not fit this." It is true, of course, and as a
result the popular favourite of to-day is well-nigh
forgotten to-morrow. In reading the critical
journals of thirty years ago it is made quite
clear that they contain few judgments which would
be sustained by a consensus of critical opinion
to-day. Whether time will deal as hardly with the
critical judgments of to-day we may not live to see.
I have no ambition to put this book to a personal
test. So far as it has any worth at all it is
meant to be bibliographical and not critical. It
aspires to furnish the young student, in handy form,
with as large a number of facts about books as can
be concentrated in so small a volume. That this
has been done under the guise of a consecutive

Introductory

narrative, and not in the form of a dictionary, is merely for the convenience of the writer.

I have endeavoured to say as little as possible about living poets and novelists. With the historians and critics the matter is of less importance. To say that Mr Samuel Rawson Gardiner has written a useful history, or that Professor David Masson's "Life of Milton" is a valuable contribution to biographical literature, will excite no antagonism. But to attempt to assign Mr W. B. Yeats a place among the poets, or "Mark Rutherford" a position among the prose writers of the day, is to trespass upon ground which it is wiser to leave to the critics who write in the literary journals from week to week. It was not possible to ignore all living writers. I have ignored as many as I dared.

It was my intention at first to devote a chapter to Sixty Years of American Literature. But for that task an Englishman who has paid but one short visit to the United States has no qualification. He can write of American literature only as seen through English eyes. That is to see much of it, it is true. Few Americans realise the enormous influence which the literature of their own land has had upon this country. Probably the most read poet in England during the sixty years has been Longfellow. Probably the most read novel has been "Uncle Tom's Cabin." Among people

Introductory

who claim to be distinctly literary Hawthorne has
been all but the favourite novelist, Washington
Irving not the least popular of essayists, and
Emerson the most invigorating moral influence.
In my youth "The Wide, Wide World" and
"Queechy" were in everybody's hands; as the
stories of Bret Harte, William Dean Howells,
Thomas Bailey Aldrich, Frank Stockton, Henry
James, and Mary Wilkins are to-day. Apart from
Dickens, nearly all our laughter has come from
Mark Twain and Artemus Ward.

In history, we in England have read Prescott
and Motley; in poetry we have read Walt Whit-
man, William Cullen Bryant, John Greenleaf
Whittier, and, above all, James Russell Lowell,
who endeared himself to us alike as a poet, a
critic, and in his own person when he represented
the United States at the Court of St James's.
Lastly I recall the delight with which as a boy I
read the "Autocrat of the Breakfast Table," and
the joy with which as a man I visited the author,
Dr Oliver Wendell Holmes, in his pleasant study
in Beacon Street, Boston. These and many other
writers have made America and the Americans
very dear to Englishmen, and this in spite of
much wild and foolish talk in the journals of the
two countries.

I have to thank Mr William Mackenzie, the
well-known publisher of Glasgow, for kindly letting

Introductory

me draw upon some articles which I wrote for his
"National Cyclopædia" ten years ago, and upon
the literary section, which he and his editor, Mr
John Brabner, permitted me to contribute at that
time to a book entitled "The Victorian Empire."
I have also to thank my friends, Dr Robertson
Nicoll and Mr L. F. Austin, for kindly reading
my proof-sheets, Mr Edward Clodd for valuable
suggestions, and Mr Sydney Webb, a friend of
old student days, for reading the chapter which
treats briefly of sociology and economics.

A compilation of this kind can scarcely hope to
escape the defects of most such enterprises—errors
both of date and of fact. I shall be glad to receive corrections for the next edition.

CLEMENT K. SHORTER.

September 27, 1897.

CHAPTER I

The Poets

WHEN Queen Victoria came to the throne in
1837, most of the great poets who had been
inspired by the French Revolutionary epoch were
dead. Keats had died in Rome in 1821, Shelley
was drowned in the Gulf of Spezzia in 1822, Byron
died at Missolonghi in 1824, Scott at Abbotsford
in 1832, and Coleridge at Highgate in 1834.
Southey was Poet Laureate, although Wordsworth
held a paramount place, recognised on all hands
as the greatest poet of the day.

The gulf which separates the Southey of the 1774-1843
laureateship from the Southey who presents himself to our judgment to-day is almost impossible
to bridge over. Southey, as the average bookman
thinks of him now, is the author of a "Life of
Nelson" and of one or two lyrics and ballads.[1]
The "Life of Nelson" is constantly republished for
an age keenly bent on Nelson worship, but for the

[1] As, for example, *The Battle of Blenheim*, *The Inchcape
Rock* and *The Cataract of Lodore.*

exacting it has been superseded by at least two biographies from living authors.[1] That Southey should live mainly by a book which was merely a publisher's commission, and not by the works which he and his contemporaries deemed immortal, is one of the ironies of literature. Southey's "Cowper" is a much better biography than his "Nelson," but in Cowper the world has almost ceased to be interested. It does not now read "Table Talk" and "The Task" any more than it reads "Thalaba" and "Madoc," although every cultivated household of sixty years ago could talk freely of these poems. There will probably be a revival of interest in Cowper. It is safe to assume that there will never be a revival of interest in Southey, and that his very lengthy poems are doomed to oblivion.

And yet it is interesting to note where Southey's contemporaries placed him. Shelley thought "Thalaba" magnificent, and its influence was marked in "Queen Mab." Coleridge spoke of its "pastoral charm." Landor found "Madoc" superb. Scott said that he had read it three or four times with ever-increasing admiration. It kept Charles James Fox out of bed till the small

[1] "The Nelson Memorial," by J. K. Laughton, 1896. "The Life of Nelson. The embodiment of the Sea Power of Great Britain," by Captain A. T. Mahan, 1897.

hours! But inexorable time has declared that these poems have no permanent place in literature. Time, however, has left us a kindly memory of Southey the man. Sara Coleridge's assertion that he was " on the whole the best man she had ever known," tallies with the judgment of many others of his contemporaries—who did not come into collision with his relentless prejudices.

Relentless prejudice was equally a characteristic of Southey's greater successor as Poet Laureate. **William Wordsworth** had written all the poems **1770-1850** by which he will live when the Queen came to the throne, but further recognition awaited the author of " Lyrical Ballads " and " Laodamia " in the thirteen years of his life that were yet to come. It was in 1839 that Keble, as Professor of Poetry at Oxford, welcomed Wordsworth when he received the honorary degree of D.C.L. with the eulogy that he had "shed a celestial light upon the affections, the occupations and the piety of the poor." In 1842 he obtained an annuity from the Civil List, and in the following year he succeeded Southey as laureate. The mere fact, however, that Wordsworth wrote nothing of importance in the present reign does not permit of his dismissal as a pre-Victorian author. His real influence, splendid and serene, was made upon the age which is passing away.

Sixty Years of

He found us when the age had bound
Our souls in its benumbing round ;
He spoke, and loosed our heart in tears.

During the period in which Wordsworth's poems were coming from the press he was scoffed at alike by Byron and by the authors of "Rejected Addresses," and they appealed to a sympathetic audience.   Coleridge had, indeed, praised him generously enough, but the author of "The Ode to Duty" knew nothing of the enthusiastic partisanship which was to be his lot in the later years of his life, and for more than a quarter of a century after his death.   I have before me two books which will serve to indicate the high-water-mark of Wordsworth's popularity.   One is a volume of selections from his poems, which was edited by Mr Matthew Arnold,[1] the other, a volume of Transactions of the Wordsworth Society, which was privately issued to the members.   In his little volume of "Selections" Mr Arnold, then recognised on all hands as our most important living critic, insisted upon Wordsworth's pre-eminence in poetry, placing him indeed on a level with Shakspere and Milton, and assigning to Byron and Shelley a secondary rank.

Mr Arnold, as events proved, only echoed a

[1] "Select Poems of Wordsworth," by Matthew Arnold. "Golden Treasury Series."

Victorian Literature

pervading sentiment. The Wordsworth Society was founded, with the Archbishop of Canterbury, the Dean of St Paul's, the Lord Chief Justice of England, the then American Minister—Mr Lowell—and a number of distinguished literary men, among its members. The Transactions of that Society give evidence that among the thoughtful men and women of the last decade Wordsworth was by far the strongest influence, that he was not merely a literary tradition, but that he was a vital force in the minds and hearts of nearly all the most interesting people of the period. Students of to-day, however, will be well content to read Wordsworth only in Matthew Arnold's "Selections." Here they will find him as a sonneteer proclaiming liberty with scarcely less zeal and power than Milton. They will find him as the sympathetic friend of the poor and of the oppressed. To be dead to the charm of Matthew Arnold's "Selections from Wordsworth" is to care nothing for poetry. To appreciate with any measure of enthusiasm the twelve volumes of Wordsworth's collected writings is equally to have one's sense of true poetry deadened and destroyed. We have no time now for "The Excursion" and "The Prelude." We have less for Wordsworth's "Ecclesiastical Sonnets" and "The Borderers." For his copious prose moralizings one has no toleration whatever.

Sixty Years of

1809-1892 It is not easy to judge whether **Alfred Tennyson** will ever cease to retain the very wide hold upon the public which was his for at least thirty years prior to his death, and which is his to-day. The poems of Tennyson might be read by succeeding generations of Englishmen if only for their exquisite purity of style. Music he has also in abundance. In "Harold," "Queen Mary," and his other plays there is no great gift of characterisation, and these assuredly will go the way of Southey's more ambitious poems. But in "Maud" Tennyson caught the social aspiration of his time with singular insight. The world, he pleaded—and England in particular—was given over to money-getting. The capitalist was more tyrannical than the old, expiring slave-owner. Even peace was a mere word. There was a worse tyranny than that which left men for dead on the battle-field. There was the tyranny which ground them to dust for a bare pittance in mill and factory. Tennyson never wrote with greater force or with more perfect dramatic and lyric art, and his poem is as striking and effective to-day as at the time of its publication in 1855.

Lord Tennyson—for the Poet Laureate accepted a peerage in 1890—won the hearts of a wider audience by "In Memoriam," and of a still larger one by "The Idylls of the King." "In Memoriam," a

lengthy elegy on his college friend, Arthur Hallam,
touched the great religious public of England.
The poem reflected a certain transcendentalism of
view which was fast becoming fashionable.

> " There lives more faith in honest doubt,
> Believe me, than in half the creeds "

was, in fact, more and more the prevailing tone
among all phases of Protestantism where a few years
earlier the exact opposite had been insisted upon.

One of the most agreeable pictures which our
literary period affords is offered by the friendship
between Lord Tennyson and Robert Browning.
The two men were not seldom compared ;
each had his partisans, and each his enthusiastic disciples. Neither from a social nor
from a literary point of view would they seem
to have had much in common. Browning was
a regular diner-out, he appeared systematically at
every picture-gallery, and at every public entertainment, and in all these things he was keenly interested : he loved society. Lord Tennyson, on
the other hand, lived a retired life in one or other
of his country houses. He was morbidly sensitive
to the attentions of the crowd, and amusing stories
are told of his desire to avoid the " vulgar " gaze.
Considered as literary men, the contrast between
these poets was greater. Tennyson's language was

dainty, simple, full of grace ; his characters monotonous, lacking in vigour. Browning wrote with rugged force, and sometimes with an obscurity which left the reader bewildered. But his gift of characterisation was superb, and his men and women for individuality are comparable only to those of Shakspere. The hearts of all of us go out to Tennyson when we think of the music of his verses, of his gifts of natural description, his fine and captivating imagination ; but our hearts and our intellects go out to Browning, as to one who has enshrined our best thoughts, who has touched all our deepest emotions. It is true that half of Browning's sixteen volumes are flatly incomprehensible to the majority of us ; but the other half are equal in bulk to the whole of Lord Tennyson's writings, and quite free from any suspicion of obscurity. The "Ring and the Book" is not obscure. It is an exciting story, dramatically told. So also are the poems called "Men and Women," and the "Dramatic Idyls." "Luria," "In a Balcony," "A Blot in the 'Scutcheon," are as readable as railway novels. And yet Browning had, and has, none of the popularity of Tennyson. The one writer sold by thousands, and his financial reward was probably unprecedented in poetry ; the other had but a small audience, an audience which never approached to one-third of his rival's. Notwithstanding all this, it is pleasing to note that the two poets loyally esteemed one another, as the dedication of some of their books conspicuously proves.

To write thus early of **Robert Browning** is to 1812-1889 anticipate in the literary record. "Pauline," the poet's first poem, was published, it is true, in 1833; and that and successive poems were accepted by good critics as the work of a true poet. Nevertheless, Browning had to fight his way as no poet of equal merit has ever had to do, and it was very late indeed in the Victorian epoch that he became more than the poet of a limited circle. One there was, certainly, who appreciated his work from the first with no common fervour, for the world has long been familiar with the statement that a reference by Elizabeth Barrett in " Lady Geraldine's Courtship" first brought the two poets together in 1845—

> " From Browning some ' Pomegranate '
> Which, if cut deep down the middle,
> Shows a heart within blood-tinctured,
> Of a veined humanity."

They were married a year later. As exemplifying the condescension of their earlier contemporaries it is interesting to note Wordsworth's observation on the event—and Wordsworth had no humour— "So, Robert Browning and Elizabeth Barrett have gone off together! Well, I hope they may understand each other—nobody else could!" Lord

Granville, who was staying in Florence when a son was born to the poets there in 1849, was still more amusing although equally uncritical. " Now there are not two incomprehensibles but three incomprehensibles," he said.

It cannot be charged against **Elizabeth Barrett** 1806-1861 **Browning** that she was in the least incomprehensible. Her " Cry of the Children," " Cowper's Grave," and " Aurora Leigh," have the note of extreme simplicity. Nor is obscurity a characteristic of " Sonnets from the Portuguese," which were not translations, but so named to disguise a wife's devotion to her husband. " Aurora Leigh " she styled a "novel in verse," and it was in fact a very readable romance, marked by that zest for social reform which characterised the period.[1] " The most mature of my works, and the one into which my highest convictions upon Life and Art have entered," she wrote of it.

After the marriage the pair lived principally at Florence. In their Florentine home—Casa Guidi —" Aurora Leigh," and " Casa Guidi Windows " were written, and here Mrs Browning died in June 1861. One may still see the house upon which the Florentine municipality has inscribed a tablet in gratitude for the " golden ring " of

[1] Charles Kingsley's " Two Years Ago " appeared the same year—in 1857.

poetry with which the enthusiastic woman poet had attempted to unite England and Italy.

Another great Florentine by adoption, **Walter Savage Landor**, came to live near the Brownings. **1775-1864** His rugged nature must have been not a little soothed by the gentle little woman with "a soul of fire enclosed in a shell of pearl." Landor was educated at Rugby, at Ashbourne, and at Trinity College, Oxford. From Rugby he was removed to avoid expulsion, and at Oxford he was rusticated. All this was the outcome of an excitable temperament, which led in later life to domestic complications, and to exile from his family in Florence. It found no reflection in his many beautiful works. As a poet, however, Landor holds no considerable rank, although here placed among them. "Gebir" was published in 1798 and "Count Julian" in 1812. Both these lengthy poems have received the rapturous praise of authoritative critics, De Quincey even declaring that Count Julian was a creation worthy to rank beside the Prometheus of Æschylus and Milton's Satan. Southey insisted indeed that Landor had written verses "of which he would rather have been the author than of any produced in our time." But Landor's poems, although obtainable in his collected works, and published in selections, command no audience to-day. With his prose the case is otherwise.

There is little in the six volumes of "Imaginary Conversations," or in the two volumes of "Longer Prose Works," that does not merit attention alike for style and matter. "Give me," he says in one of his prefaces, "ten accomplished men for readers and I am content." Landor has all accomplished men for readers now. And all are at one with the critic who said that, "excepting Shakspere, no other writer has furnished us with so many delicate aphorisms of human nature." Mr Swinburne's expression of veneration is well known.

> " I came as one whose thoughts half linger,
>   Half run before ;
> The youngest to the oldest singer
>   That England bore.
>
> I found him whom I shall not find
>   Till all grief end ;
> In holiest age our mightiest mind,
>   Father and friend."

The connecting link between Landor and his young admirer is sufficiently apparent. In genuine accomplishment, the imaginative literature of our era has produced no one comparable to Landor, save only **Algernon Charles Swinburne**. Mr Swinburne has written well in several languages other than his own. In his own he has written tragedies of wider purpose than those of Tennyson, of equal insight with those of Browning. He has written

1837-

noble sonnets, lyrics of exquisite melody, and one poem, "Ave atque Vale," which takes rank among the imperishable elegies of our literature. He has abundant spontaneity and a marvellous gift of rhythm. Added to all this, he is a critic of almost unequalled learning and distinction. He was the first to give adequate recognition to the poetic genius of Matthew Arnold and Emily Brontë. He knows Elizabethan literature with remarkable thoroughness, and he knows the literature of many ages and many lands better than most of the professors. His appreciation of Charles Lamb endears him to English readers, and his eulogies of Victor Hugo command the respect of Frenchmen. A great poet and a great prose writer, Mr Swinburne is perhaps the most distinguished literary figure of our day. Only when in the distant years his country has lost him, will a great folly be generally recognised. Why, it will be asked, did we not spontaneously call for him — arch democrat and arch rebel though he may have been—as the only possible successor to Lord Tennyson as Poet Laureate?

It has been said that Mr Swinburne was the first to recognise the great poetical gifts of **Matthew Arnold**. Writing in the *Fortnightly Review* in **1822-1888** 1867,[1] he remarked that the fame of Mr Matthew

---

[1] Reprinted in 1875 in "Essays and Studies."

Arnold had for some years been almost exclusively the fame of a prose writer. "Those students," he continued, "could hardly find hearing, who with all esteem and enjoyment of his essays . . . retained the opinion that, if justly judged, he must be judged by his verse and not by his prose." The view that Arnold excelled as a prose writer continued to hold sway for many years after Mr Swinburne wrote, and it was current up to the date of Arnold's death. "Literature and Dogma" and "God and the Bible," the former of which first appeared in 1873, excited an extraordinary amount of attention, and helped largely to modify the religious beliefs of many men and women now rapidly approaching middle age. The son of a famous clergyman, Dr Thomas Arnold of Rugby, Matthew Arnold was a product of that Broad Church movement which Dr Arnold had helped largely to inspire. A fellow-pupil of Dr Stanley, Dean of Westminster, Arnold went further than the Dean in his opposition to supernaturalism in religion, though he stopped short of the fiery antagonism which another eminent Anglican churchman, Bishop Colenso, displayed towards the miraculous stories of the Old Testament. But far more than Stanley or Colenso did he influence the Protestant Christianity of his day. This, however, scarcely enters into the discussion of Matthew Arnold the poet. More akin to that

Victorian Literature

side of Arnold's life is his literary criticism. For many years he held in this field a well nigh undisputed throne. For a time he was Professor of Poetry at Oxford. But his influence came mainly through a volume called "Essays in Criticism" (1865), of which it is not too much to say that the paper entitled "The Function of Criticism at the Present Time," gave a new impulse to all students of books. Here and elsewhere Arnold emphasised the opinion that not only a fine artistic instinct but a vast amount of knowledge, admitting of comparisons, is necessary as the equipment of a critic. Criticism he defined as "a disinterested endeavour to learn and propagate the best that is known and thought in the world." Matthew Arnold had other claims as a prose writer. His appeal for the study of Celtic literature initiated and encouraged a revival of learning in Wales and in Ireland; and his books and essays on Education—for his main income for many years was derived from his salary as an Inspector of Schools—did much to further the cause which his brother-in-law, Mr W. E. Forster, began with the great Education Act of 1870.

But it is as a poet, as Mr Swinburne foretold, that Matthew Arnold lives in literature. It is strange to some of us to note how largely the bulk of his prose work has dropped out of the memory of the younger generation. The diligent collector possesses some forty-five volumes of Mr Arnold's writings; but although there has been a cheap reprint of many of these, it is only by his collected poems that he is widely known to-day. Mr Swinburne, in the essay to which I have referred, tells of the joy with which, as a schoolboy, he came upon a copy of "Empedocles on Etna." He must then have been about fifteen years of age, as "Empedocles on Etna and Other Poems by A" was published in 1852. It contained "Tristram and Iseult," "Stanzas in Memory of the Author of 'Obermann,'" and many now accepted favourites. "The Strayed Reveller" by "A" was a still earlier volume of anonymous verse (1849); and, in 1853, "Poems" by Matthew Arnold made the poet known by name to a small circle. A substantial recognition as a poet did not however fall to Matthew Arnold while he lived. His career is, indeed, a striking example of the fact that our views of contemporary literature require to be revised every decade. Ten years ago everyone was discussing Matthew Arnold's views concerning Isaiah and St Paul, and the Nonconformists, whom he chaffed good-humouredly, have reconstructed many of their beliefs through a study of his works. People were excited by his views on education and by his views on literature, but not by his poetry. To-day his poetry is all of him that remains, and its charm is likely to soothe

the more strenuous minds among us for at least another generation, and perhaps for all time.

In "Thyrsis," a striking elegy on **Arthur Hugh Clough**, Arnold struck a note which has only **1819-1861** Milton's "Lycidas" and Shelley's "Adonais" to call forth comparisons. Clough was not a Keats, but he was a more considerable personage than Milton's friend, and indeed he has been persistently underrated by many men of letters. Not indeed by all. "We have a foreboding," said Mr Lowell, "that Clough will be thought a hundred years hence, to have been the truest expression in verse of the moral and intellectual tendencies of the period in which he lived." Clough was the son of a cotton merchant of Liverpool, and he was a pupil of Dr Arnold at Rugby. He gained a Balliol scholarship and went into residence in 1837. The coming years brought doubts and distractions, religious and political, and Clough parted from Oxford. His most famous poem, "The Bothie of Tober-na-Vuolich," was published in 1848. In 1852 he sailed to Boston in the same ship that carried Thackeray and Lowell. Emerson, who had met him in England, welcomed him there. Travelling through Europe for his health, he died of paralysis in Florence in 1861.[1]

[1] See "Poems and Prose Remains" by Arthur Hugh Clough, with a Selection from his Letters, and a Memoir, edited by his wife. 2 vols., 1888.

Sixty Years of

The catalogue of great English poets of the period is completed with the names of Rossetti and Morris. Perhaps there is no more romantic figure in modern literature than **Dante Gabriel** 1828-1882 **Rossetti,** although he has suffered cruelly from the biographer. His father, Gabriele, was an Italian exile, a critic of Dante, a teacher of Italian in London. His mother was a sister of the notorious Polidori, whose charlatanry is remembered wherever an interest in Lord Byron prevails.

The younger Rossetti had relatives—a brother, William Michael, who has written verses, criticisms, and a ponderous biography of Gabriel; and a sister, 1827-1876 **Maria Francesca Rossetti,** whose "Shadow of Dante" makes good reading for admirers of the great Florentine, and, indeed, may be recommended to every English student of Dante. Another sister, 1830-1894 **Christina Georgina Rossetti,** wrote many books. She will live by her "Goblin Market" (1862), and by numerous short poems. Books of the type of "Called to be Saints" and "The Face of the Deep: A Commentary on the Revelation," have also won her much affection and admiration from religious sympathisers. She was not responsible for "Maude" and "New Poems," inadequate works which her brother thought fit to publish after her death. They are practically worthless.

Dante Rossetti was a considerable painter as well as a poet. His name is written large in that pre-

Victorian Literature

Raphaelite movement which gave him for associates Mr Holman Hunt and Sir John Millais. The movement, which had Mr John Ruskin for its literary champion, when reduced to simple statement, meant a harking back to early mediæval art. Sir John Millais and Mr Holman Hunt speedily abandoned this position, and Rossetti himself was never a pre-Raphaelite in any real sense. The pre-Raphaelites issued in 1850 a journal under the editorship of Rossetti's brother, and to the *Germ*, as it was called, Rossetti contributed his poem, "The Blessed Damozel," and a story, "Hand and Soul." To the *Germ* also, Thomas Woolner (1825-1892), the sculptor, contributed the poems of "My Beautiful Lady."

One epoch in the life of Rossetti was his introduction to Mr Ruskin, and another was his first acquaintance with William Morris. Ruskin bought his pictures with characteristic generosity, and further assisted Rossetti to publish "The Early Italian Poets" (1861), afterwards reprinted as "Dante and his Circle" (1874). William Morris introduced Rossetti to his Oxford friends, including Mr Swinburne, and to the *Oxford and Cambridge Magazine*, in which many of his finest poems were published. After his wife's death, from an overdose of laudanum in 1862, Rossetti moved to Queen's House, Cheyne Walk, where for a time he had for associates in payment of rent Mr Swinburne and Mr George Meredith, though the latter never actually lived in the house. From that time to his death he published many important poems—ballads of singular power like "The White Ship," "The King's Tragedy," and "Sister Helen," and the many splendid sonnets of "The House of Life." The two volumes of Rossetti's collected works must always command readers. Rossetti died at Birchington-on-Sea, and a simple tomb in the churchyard marks his grave.

1834-1896 The name of **William Morris** closes the list of Victorian poets of the first rank. Morris was as versatile as Rossetti. He touched many branches of Art with remarkable success. Now he was designing wall-papers, and became a successful manufacturer in this branch of commerce : now he was indefatigable in printing notable books in English literature from a type which he had himself selected. The wall-paper has given a new direction to the decoration of English houses, and the Kelmscott Press has added many beautiful books to our libraries, and given an impetus to a revival of taste in printing. This was but a part of Morris's life. Although a rich man, he was a vigorous lecturer on behalf of Socialism, and wrote many books, such as, for example : "The Dream of John Ball " (1888), and "News from Nowhere "

Victorian Literature

(1891), in support of his ideals. From the appearance of his "Defence of Guenevere" (1858), and "Life and Death of Jason" (1867), he was always publishing, and his translations from Homer, Virgil, and Scandinavian literature make a small library by themselves. But a practical handbook to Victorian literature needs but to mention one of his books. "The Earthly Paradise" (1868-70), will live as long as a love of good story-telling remains to us. The tales are told by twenty-four travellers who desire to find the earthly paradise, and the book opens as do the Canterbury Tales with a Prologue. The lyrical introduction is one of the most quotable things in our later literature :—

" Of Heaven or Hell I have no power to sing,
    I cannot ease the burden of your fears,
    Or make quick-coming death a little thing.
    Or bring again the pleasure of past years,
    Nor for my words shall ye forget your tears,
    Or hope again for aught that I can say,
    The idle singer of an empty day.

" Dreamer of dreams, born out of my due time,
    Why should I strive to set the crooked straight?
    Let it suffice me that my murmuring rhyme
    Beats with light wing against the ivory gate,
    Telling a tale not too importunate
    To those who in the sleepy region stay,
    Lulled by the singer of an empty day.

" Folk say, a wizard to a Northern King
  At Christmastide such wondrous things did show
  That through one window men beheld the Spring,
  And through another saw the Summer glow,
  And through a third the fruited vines arow,
  While still, unheard, but in its wonted way,
  Piped the drear wind of that December day."

William Morris has not seldom been confused with a writer with whom he had nothing in common but the name. **Sir Lewis Morris**, a Welsh squire, and candidate for Parliament, has stood for convention as decisively as William Morris has stood against it. His " Songs of Two Worlds " (1871-5), and " Epic of Hades " (1876), brought him a considerable popularity, which " A Vision of Saints," and later books have not been able to maintain. Another literary knight of our time who has secured a large share of public attention through his verse is **Sir Edwin Arnold**, whose " Light of Asia " interpreted to many the story of Buddha's career. A poem upon Christ and Christianity " The Light of the World," owed the fact of its smaller success to the greater familiarity of the public with its main incidents. Sir Edwin Arnold has won other laurels as a traveller and as a journalist.

Some of the best poetry of the era has been produced by writers whose principal achievements are in the realm of prose. The Brontës,

Victorian Literature

Charles Kingsley, George Meredith, and George
Eliot—to name but a few—all wrote verse which
must ultimately have secured attention had they
not made great reputations as novelists.

Assuredly, the three most successful poems in
Victorian literature, of that portion of it which is
already passing into oblivion, are "Proverbial
Philosophy," "Festus," and "Philip Van Artevelde." The "Proverbial Philosophy" of **Martin
Farquhar Tupper** created an excitement in literary **1810-1889**
and non-literary circles, which it is difficult for the
present generation to comprehend. It is true that
when it was first published, in 1838, it was greeted
by the *Athenaeum* as "a book not likely to please
beyond the circle of a few minds as eccentric as
the author's." In spite of this, it sold in thousands
and hundreds of thousands; it went through over
nine hundred editions in England, and five
hundred thousand copies at least were sold in
America. It was translated into French, German,
and many other tongues; its author was a popular
hero, although of his later books, including "Ballads for the Times," "Raleigh, his Life and
Death," and "Cithara," the very names are
by this time forgotten. Of "Proverbial Philosophy" itself there are few enough copies in
demand to-day, and it is difficult for us to
place ourselves in the position of those who felt
its charm. What to the early Victorian Era

was counted for wisdom, and piety, and even for beauty, counts to the present age for mere commonplace verbiage. Tupper's name has taken a place in our language as the contemptuous synonym for a poetaster. "Festus," on the other hand, although not read to-day, has always commanded respectful attention. Its author, **Philip James Bailey**, wrote "Festus" in its first form, at the age of twenty, and it was published in 1839. The book was enlarged again and again, till it reached to three times its original length. It may be that this enlargement has had something to do with its fate. "Festus" was frequently compared to the best work of Goethe and of Mr Browning. Even a more pronounced recognition accrued to the dramatic poems of **Sir Henry Taylor**, and more particularly to "Philip Van Artevelde" (1834), which was described by the *Quarterly Review* as "the noblest effort in the true old taste of our English historical drama, that has been made for more than a century," and which attracted the keenest attention of all Sir Henry Taylor's contemporaries. His entertaining "Autobiography" has told us that Taylor, who was an important official at the Colonial Office, knew all the famous men of his time.

Women have occupied no small share in the literary history of the past sixty years, although

1816-

1800-1886

Victorian Literature

it is in fiction that their most enduring triumphs
have been secured. The most popular women
poets, next in order to Mrs Browning, have been
Eliza Cook and Jean Ingelow. **Eliza Cook** wrote **1818-1889**
for the most part the kind of verses which would
now be rejected by the editor of the Poet's Corner
of a provincial newspaper. She would be little
more than a vague memory, were it not for
" The Old Arm-Chair " ; but she has other
claims to consideration. In the forties and the
fifties *Eliza Cook's Journal* was one of the most
prominent publications of the day, and it did
much for the cause of literature and philan-
thropy. **Jean Ingelow** survived, as did Eliza Cook, **1820-1897**
to see her verse well-nigh forgotten, and yet it is
stated that two hundred thousand copies of her
poems have been sold in America alone. Miss
Ingelow, who was born in Boston, Lincolnshire,
and died in London, will live in anthologies by
her ballad, " High Tide on the Coast of Lincolnshire," by a song in "Supper at the Mill," and
by sundry short poems.

A certain brighter and more humorous kind of
verse had its beginnings with Thomas Hood and the
author of " The Ingoldsby Legends." **Thomas Hood** **1798-1845**
has endeared himself to the whole reading world
by his " Song of the Shirt" (1844); and his "Dream
of Eugene Aram " (1829) is not less familiar. But

in addition to this he had an abundance of wit and drollery side by side with pathos and tenderness, which will always make a splendid tradition and a great inspiration. Hood was a journalist. His prototype, **Richard Harris Barham**, was an Anglican clergyman. His pseudonym of Thomas Ingoldsby calls up memories of some of the quaintest and drollest verse ever written. "The Ingoldsby Legends" were first contributed to *Bentley's Miscellany*, and afterwards collected in volumes. "The Jackdaw of Rheims" is the most popular. Barham's once successful novel, "My Cousin Nicholas," is now all but forgotten.

1788-1845

The most famous successors of Hood and Barham have been Calverley and Mr Austin Dobson. **Charles Stuart Calverley** wrote "Fly Leaves" and "Verses and Translations." Mr Dobson has published, in addition to many valuable prose works, the exquisite "Vignettes in Rhyme" and "Proverbs in Porcelain," which, with Mr Andrew Lang's "Ballades in Blue China," form a dainty contribution to the lighter literature of the epoch.

1831-1884

A determination to say as little as possible concerning writers still young in years, though already famous, will make, it may be, my summary of Victorian poetry seem inadequate to many. Mr Traill, a discerning critic, has specified some hundred or more "minor poets" who flourish to-day! But

it cannot be doubted that the minor poet of our era,
with his excellent technique, his deep feeling, and his
high-minded impulsiveness, is separated by an immense gulf from the minor poet of an earlier period.
The Pyes and the Hayleys, who were famous in
an age when criticism was less of an art, had little
enough of the real poetical faculty. That faculty can
scarcely be denied to the hundred or more of living
bards who now claim the suffrages of the poetry-
loving reader.   It cannot be denied also to many
men who have passed away during the present
era—to Alexander Smith and Sydney Dobell in
one period, and to Coventry Patmore and
James Thomson in another.   **Alexander Smith** 1830-1867
was an industrious essayist as well as a poet.
Tennyson and Mrs Browning concurred in their
esteem of Smith as a poet "whose works show
fancy, and not imagination"; and this might with
truth be said of too many of the minor bards, and,
indeed, constitutes the dividing line.   Sydney
Yendys, under which pseudonym **Sydney Dobell** 1824-1874
co-operated with Smith in "Sonnets on the War"
(1855), was a poet of similar temperament.

Coventry Patmore is known to the many 1823-1896
through his "Angel in the House," a poem upon
domestic bliss which breathed a note not always
sincere, but to which Mr Ruskin assured a certain popularity through effective quotation in his

"Sesame and Lilies." A certain ecstatic band of admirers attached more importance to Patmore's "Unknown Eros." These admirers spoilt him by adulation. He probably looked forward with the same keen assurance to the verdict of posterity as did Southey; and posterity it is all but certain will be as ruthless in the one case as in the other.

Patmore's life was one of luxury and independence. Quite the reverse was the fate of **James** 1834-1882 **Thomson,** whose great poem, "The City of Dreadful Night," was published in Mr Charles Bradlaugh's *National Reformer* in 1874, and not republished as a book until 1880. Thomson had a melancholy career which ended in drink and disaster. He died in University Hospital, London. His "City of Dreadful Night" is peculiarly a reflection of the age that is passing. It secured even during the poet's life the commendation of George Eliot, of George Meredith, and of other critics; and it may yet command a large audience, who breathe the note of pessimism which was always characteristic of the writer :—

" The sense that every struggle brings defeat
    Because Fate holds no prize to crown success,
That all the oracles are dumb or cheat
    Because they have no secret to express ;
That none can pierce the vast black veil uncertain
Because there is no light beyond the curtain;
That all is vanity and nothingness."

Victorian Literature

A poet whom one names with peculiar reverence is **Thomas Aubrey de Vere**, the son of Sir Aubrey 1814- de Vere, who was also a poet. Aubrey de Vere, the younger, knew and loved Wordsworth, to whom in 1842 he dedicated "The Waldenses : A Lyrical Tale," and yet retains, sixty years later, the most sympathetic interest in modern literary effort. Mr de Vere is an Irishman, and was educated at Trinity College, Dublin. He has written many volumes of poetry and prose, his dramatic poems "Alexander the Great" and "St Thomas of Canterbury" having, no doubt, been largely inspired by the successes of his friend and relative, Sir Henry Taylor, and by his father's brilliant drama, "Mary Tudor." One of his most recent books was a volume of critical essays containing a notable study of Wordsworth.

Irishmen have been fairly conspicuous in the poetry of the epoch, and the term "Celtic Renaissance" has begun to be used hopefully by lovers of Ireland who desire that country to have a literature as distinctly Irish as Scotland has a literature definitely Scottish. **Thomas Moore** was the pioneer of this move- 1779-1852 ment. He had, it is true, done all his work before the Queen came to the throne, although he lived yet another fifteen years. His "Irish Melodies" began to appear in 1807, "Lalla

Rookh" was published in 1817, and the "Life of Byron" in 1830. Moore was as much an inspiration to modern Ireland as Burns to modern Scotland, and the one country holds the name of its poet as reverentially in memory as does the other. Moore, however, lacked the note of passionate sincerity which pertained to Burns; although we may fairly ask what would have been the career of Burns had he been thrown early into the literary and social life of London—the London of Byron's time.

The influence of Moore was strong in **Thomas** 1814-1845 **Davis** whose "National and Historical Ballads, Songs and Poems" caused so great a ferment in the heart of Young Ireland. Many other Irish writers deserve to be named, such as James Clarence Mangan (1803-1849), Sir Samuel Ferguson (1810-1886), Lady Dufferin (1807-1867) and John Banim (1798-1842), who wrote, in conjunction with his brother Michael, some twenty-four volumes of Irish stories and verses. **Samuel** 1797-1868 **Lover** is best known in England by his romance "Rory O'More" and his ever popular "Handy Andy," but in Ireland he is remembered as a writer of lyrics and ballads of heart-stirring character.

An Irishman by descent, although not by birth, 1809-1883 was **Edward FitzGerald**, who was born in Suffolk

and lived all his life in the neighbourhood of Wood-
bridge in that county. FitzGerald's " Letters and
Literary Remains " fill three substantial volumes,
but he lives for us by his translation or rather
paraphrase of the " Rubáyát of Omar Khayyám
of Naishápur," which first appeared in 1859. It
is generally agreed that FitzGerald, a nineteenth
century pagan, always reverently questioning the
mystery of existence, superadded his own personal thoughts and feelings to the verses of the
old Persian singer. In doing this he touched
deeply a certain aspect of the second half of the
nineteenth century and founded a cult. Fitz-
Gerald's verses, however, have been ardently
admired by many who are far from accepting
their pessimist view of life.

Hartley Coleridge wrote and published his **1796-1849**
admirable sonnets before 1837. He was a
son of Samuel Taylor Coleridge (1772-1834),
whose literary remains were edited by Henry
Nelson Coleridge, a nephew and son-in-law. H.
N. Coleridge married the great poet's only daughter,
Sara Coleridge, who wrote one poem, " Phantas- **1803-1852**
mion," and whose letters throw much light on an
important chapter of literary history.

Bryan Waller Procter, better known as " Barry **1787-1874**
Cornwall," was at school with Lord Byron at

Harrow. His "Dramatic Scenes," "Marcian Colonna," and "Mirandola" were much talked of in their day. Procter was admired as a poet by Byron, Moore, and other famous contemporaries, but no one reads him now. A happier fate has 1825-1864 befallen his daughter, **Adelaide Anne Procter,** whose "Legends and Lyrics" are still widely popular.

Winthrop Mackworth Praed, who wrote much admirable humorous and satirical verse, is not a Victorian author, although his present popularity makes that rather hard to realise. He died in 1803-1884 1839. **Richard Hengist Horne,** on the other hand, although he lived into our time, is now remembered only by his friendship with Mrs Browning and by the humorous freak of publishing his epic "Orion" at a farthing. He was the author of a miracle play entitled "Judas Iscariot," a tragedy entitled "The Death of Marlowe," and many other works.

Another writer of well-nigh forgotten tragedies 1803-1849 was **Thomas Lovell Beddoes,** who wrote "The Bride's Tragedy" and "Death's Jest Book." A like extinction, it is to be feared, has befallen Ebenezer Jones and Ebenezer Elliott—the former of whom belonged to that spasmodic school of poets of which Alexander Smith and Philip James

36

Victorian Literature

Bailey were supposed to be the leaders. **Ebenezer Jones** wrote "Studies in Sensation and Event," to 1820-1860 which in 1879 his brother, Sumner Jones, attached an interesting biography. There is very genuine poetry in the volume, but it is not likely to be republished. **Ebenezer Elliott** had a very different 1781-1849 fate. He enjoyed for many years the suffrages of the multitude. His "Corn Law Rhymes" played a considerable part in the political agitation of the period. James Montgomery called him "the poet of the poor." Another writer with a fine democratic impulse was **Gerald Massey**, who was asso- 1828- ciated with the Chartist movement, and wrote "Poems and Charms" and "Voices of Freedom and Lyrics of Love." Another Chartist was **Thomas Cooper**, who wrote "The Purgatory of 1805-1892 Suicides" and many other poems and an entertaining autobiography. Cooper was an active political agitator, and was imprisoned for two years in Stafford gaol for sedition.

A poet who holds a great place in the minds of many is **William Barnes**, who kept a school for a 1820-1886 time in Mr Thomas Hardy's town of Dorchester. He afterwards became a clergyman and rector of Winterbourne-Came. He was a philologist as well as a poet, and published many works on language. His interest for us here is in his "Poems of Rural Life in the Dorset Dialect"

1803-1875 (1844). Another poet-clergyman of great learning was **Robert Stephen Hawker** whose work reflects Devonshire and Cornwall as Barnes' reflects Dorsetshire. He wrote the "Song of the Western Men" which he deceived Macaulay into believing to be an old Cornish ballad, and the great historian introduced it into his "History of England" as an example of the excitement caused by the arrest of the seven bishops.[1] Its stirring refrain :—

" And shall Trelawney die, and shall Trelawney die ?
   Then thirty thousand Cornish boys will know the reason
     why "

will always keep Hawker in remembrance. He was vicar of Morwenstow and wrote several volumes of poems and some prose, including "Footprints of Former Men in Far Cornwall."

Two poets, father and son, made the name of Marston honoured in their days. John Westland Marston (1819-1890) was born at Boston, Lincolnshire. He wrote two dramas, "Strathmore" and "Marie de Méranie," which had much success some years ago. Another work, "A Hard Struggle," obtained the enthusiastic praise of Dickens. Dr Garnett claims for Marston that he was long the chief upholder of the poetical drama

[1] All over the country the peasants chanted a ballad of which the burden is still remembered. MACAULAY, History, Vol. II., p. 371.

Victorian Literature

on the English stage. **Philip Bourke Marston**, a 1850-1887
son of Westland Marston, should not have failed
of literary success, as he had for godfather Philip
James Bailey, the author of "Festus," and for
godmother Miss Mulock, author of "John Hali-
fax, Gentleman." He, however, became blind at
three years of age. He published three volumes
of verse, "Song Tide and Other Poems" (1871),
"All in All" (1875) and "Wind Voices" (1883).
They were never popular, although his poetry
gained him the esteem of many eminent men,
Rossetti and Mr Swinburne among others. Mrs
Chandler Moulton, an American lady who wrote
"Swallow Flights," gave us a memoir of Philip
Bourke Marston. In this she was assisted by Mr
William Sharp, who was also one of Rossetti's biographers. Mrs Moulton did a like good office to
the memory of **Arthur O'Shaughnessy**, a poet of 1844-1881
considerable distinction in his day. O'Shaughnessy married the younger Marston's sister. His
"Epic of Women & Other Poems," published in
1870, was a volume of very great promise. He
wrote other verses, which never attained to quite
the same measure of success.

It only remains for me to name **Alfred Austin** 1835-
the Poet Laureate. After Lord Tennyson's death
in 1892 the office remained vacant for four years.
The two poets who might have been considered to

have had some claim, William Morris and Mr
Swinburne, were supposed to be impossible on
account of democratic sympathies, although it is
doubtful if either would have accepted the office.
Almost every living poet, however small the bulk
of his achievement, and however inconsiderable
his years, was nominated—by the press—in turn.
Finally, in 1896, by a pleasant irony of circumstances, the laureateship was given to a journalist,—
for Mr Austin had been a leader-writer on the staff
of the *Standard* newspaper for many years. He
has written "The Golden Age, a Satire" (1871),
"Savonarola" (1881), "English Lyrics" 1891,
and many prose works. His "English Lyrics"
contained an appreciative introduction by William
Watson, the author of "Wordsworth's Grave,"
"Lachrymæ Musarum," and other poems which
have been received with abundant cordiality by
the press and public. Another living poet who has
1864- been well and justly praised is **Rudyard Kipling**.
He made his earliest fame as a writer of short
stories of Indian military life. "Soldiers Three"
and "Wee Willie Winkie" have entirely captivated
the imagination of Mr Kipling's contemporaries.
It is as a poet, however, that he will perhaps
longest retain his hold upon them. His "Barrack-
Room Ballads" (1892) are finely touched with that
martial spirit which so strongly appeals to the heart
of our nation.

CHAPTER II

The Novelists

ANY comparison of the novels of the Victorian Era, with the novels of the Georgian Period, must be very much to the disadvantage of the former. The great epoch of English fiction began with Goldsmith and Richardson, and ended with Sir Walter Scott. It was an epoch which gave us "The Vicar of Wakefield," "Clarissa," "Tom Jones," "Pride and Prejudice," "Humphrey Clinker," and "Tristram Shandy." That fiction had a naturalness and spontaneity to which the novels of the Victorian Era can lay no claim. The novels of the period with which we are concerned aspire to regenerate mankind. Dickens, indeed, started off with but little literary equipment save sundry eighteenth century novels. He had read Smollett, and Fielding, and Sterne, diligently. But the influence of these humourists—so marked in "Pickwick"—became qualified in his succeeding books by the strenuous spirit of the times.

It is alike interesting in itself and convenient

for my purpose that the most popular novelist of the Victorian era should have published his first great book in 1837. Dickens awoke then to abundant fame, and his popularity has never waned for an instant during the sixty succeeding years. To-day he may be more or less decried by "literary" people, but his audience has multiplied twofold. He has added to it the countless thousands whom the School Board has given to the reading world.

1812-1870 **Charles Dickens** was born at Landport, Portsea, his father being an improvident clerk in the Navy Pay Office at Portsmouth. Dickens senior has been immortalized for us by the not too pleasing portrait of "Micawber." After infinite struggle and penury, Dickens became a reporter for the *Morning Chronicle.* Under the signature of "Boz" he wrote "Sketches" for the *Monthly Magazine* in 1834. "Pickwick" appeared from April 1836 to November 1837, and alike in parts and in book form took the world by storm. It was succeeded by "Oliver Twist" (1838), "Nicholas Nickleby" (1839), "The Old Curiosity Shop" (1840), and "Barnaby Rudge" (1841). From this time forth Dickens was the most popular writer that our literature has seen. Within twelve years after his death some four millions of his books were sold in England, and there is no reason to believe that this popularity has in any

Victorian Literature

way abated, although George Eliot foretold that much of Dickens's humour would be meaningless to the next generation, that is to say, to the generation which is now with us. It is the fashion to call Dickens the novelist of the half-educated, to charge him with lack of reflectiveness, with incapacity for serious reasoning. His humour has been described as insincere, his pathos as exaggerated. Much of this indictment may with equal justice be made against Richardson and even against Jane Austen, who surely anticipated Dickens by the creation of the Rev. William Collins.

If Dickens had been a learned University Professor he would not have possessed the equipment most needful for the artist who was to portray to us in an imperishable manner the London which is now fast disappearing. The people who censure Dickens are those for whom he has served a purpose and is of no further use. They are a mere drop in the ocean of readers. It is not easy to-day to gauge his precise position. The exhaustion of many of his copyrights has given up his work to a host of rival publishers. There are probably thousands of men and women now, as there were in the fifties and sixties, who have been stimulated by him, and who have found in his writings the aid to a cheery optimism which has made life more tolerable amid adverse conditions. Mrs Richmond Ritchie, Thackeray's daughter, tells us how keenly Dickens's capacity for stirring the heart was felt even in the home of the rival novelist. Thackeray's youngest daughter, then a child, looked up from the book she was reading to ask the question, " Papa, why do you not write books like ' Nicholas Nickleby ' "? Thackeray himself shared the general enthusiasm. " David Copperfield ! " he writes to a correspondent, " By Jingo ! It is beautiful ! It is charming ! Bravo Dickens ! It has some of his very brightest touches—those inimitable Dickens touches which make such a great man of him. And the reading of the book has done another author a great deal of good. . . . It has put me on my mettle and made me feel that I must do something; that I have fame and name and family to support."

If Dickens is still beloved by the multitude, 1811-1863 the name of **William Makepeace Thackeray** has entirely eclipsed his in the minds of a certain literary section of the community. Thackeray stands to them for culture, Dickens for illiteracy. Thackeray had indeed a more polished intellect; he had also a more restrained style. Thackeray was born at Calcutta. His father, who was an Indian civil servant, died when the boy was only five years old. He was educated at Charterhouse School and Trinity College, Cambridge. In 1831 he went to Weimar. He studied long at Paris

Victorian Literature

with a view to becoming an artist, and when
"Pickwick" wanted an illustrator to continue the
work of Seymour who had committed suicide,
Thackeray applied to Dickens, but Hablot Browne
was chosen, and Thackeray was disappointed—
happily for the world, which lost an indifferent
artist to gain a great author. Thackeray in 1837
—the year which saw the publication of "Pickwick" as a volume—joined the staff of *Fraser's
Magazine*. In that journal appeared in succession
"The History of Samuel Titmarsh and the
Great Hoggarty Diamond," "The Yellowplush
Papers," and "The Memoirs of Barry Lyndon."
In 1847 "Vanity Fair" was begun in numbers,
and not till then did its author secure real renown.
"Pendennis" was published in 1850, and "Es-
mond" in 1852. "The Newcomes" (1854) is in
some measure a sequel to "Pendennis," as "The
Virginians" (1858) is in some measure a sequel
to "Esmond." These are the five works by
Thackeray which everyone must read. In 1857
Thackeray unsuccessfully contested Oxford. In
1859 he undertook the editorship of the new
Cornhill Magazine which flourished in his hands.
These were the halcyon days of magazine editors.
On Macaulay's death in 1859, Thackeray talked
of purchasing the historian's vacant house. A
friend remarked upon his prosperity. "To make
money one must edit a magazine," was the answer.

He did not buy Macaulay's house, but built himself one at Palace Green, and here he died the day before Christmas-day 1863. His daughter, Anne Thackeray, who became Mrs Richmond Ritchie, has written " Old Kensington " and other stories of singular charm.

The twenty-six volumes of Thackeray's works make a veritable nursery of style for the modern literary aspirant. But it is, as has been said, upon his five great novels that his future fame must rest. They are as permanent a picture of life among the well-to-do classes as those Dickens has given us of life among the poor.

1816-1855 **Charlotte Brontë**, who gave to Thackeray the enthusiastic hero-worship of her early years, called him a Titan, and dedicated " Jane Eyre " to him, had little enough in common with the author of " Vanity Fair." The daughter of a poor parson of Irish birth, she was born at Thornton in Yorkshire. She and two sisters grew up in the cramped atmosphere of a vicarage at Haworth, in the centre of the moorlands. They wrote stories and poems from childhood, and dreamed of literary fame. Meanwhile it was necessary to add to the scanty stipend of their father ; two of them went back as governesses to the school in which they had been educated ; and all of them a little later attempted the uncongenial life of private governesses.

46

Victorian Literature

The desire to have a school of their own led
Charlotte and her sister Emily to Brussels, where
they studied French and German. Returning to
the Haworth parsonage, the three sisters, Charlotte, Emily, and Anne, with money left them by
an aunt, published a volume of verse—" Poems
by Currer, Ellis, and Acton Bell." Then each
sister produced from her drawer the manuscript
of a novel, and Charlotte's "Professor," Emily's
"Wuthering Heights," and Anne's "Agnes Grey"
were sent round to the publishers and returned
more than once to the parsonage. Finally the
"Professor" was read by Smith & Elder, who
asked for a longer story by the writer. "Jane
Eyre" (1847) was the result, and that story became one of the most successful novels of the day.
It was followed by "Shirley" (1849) and "Villette"
(1853). In 1854 Charlotte Brontë became Mrs
Arthur Bell Nicholls, and the wife of her father's
curate. In the following year she died. "The
Professor" was published two years after her death.

Emily Brontë accomplished less than her elder 1818-1848
sister, but her name will live as long. She secured
the admiration of Sydney Dobell, of Matthew
Arnold, and of Mr Swinburne, and her best verse
is perhaps the greatest ever written by a woman.
"Last Lines" and "The Old Stoic" will rank
with the finest poetry in our literature. Her one

47

novel, "Wuthering Heights," has been most happily criticised by Mr Swinburne : " As was the author's life so is her book in all things ; troubled and taintless, with little of rest in it and nothing of reproach. It may be true that not many will ever take it to their hearts ; it is certain that those who do like it will like nothing very much better in the whole world of poetry or prose."

Emily Brontë's sole contributions to literature were the poems written in conjunction with her two sisters under the name of Ellis Bell, some further poems published by her sister Charlotte after her death, and the single novel " Wuthering Heights."

1819-1849   **Anne Brontë** wrote more than her sister Emily, but with less of recognition.   She contributed verses to the little volume of poems under the name of Acton Bell, and additional verses were published after her death by Charlotte.   In addition to this she wrote two novels, the first of them "Agnes Grey," and the second "The Tenant of Wildfell Hall."   This last, curiously enough, went into a second edition during Anne's lifetime, and she contributed a preface to it defending herself against her critics.   Neither Anne's poetry nor her novels are of any account to-day. They would not be read, were it not for the glory with which her two sisters have surrounded the name of Brontë.

Victorian Literature

Women novelists have abundantly flourished during the Victorian Era, but then the path was made easy for them by Jane Austen, Maria Edgeworth, and Fanny Burney. By all those who delight in debatable comparisons the name of George Eliot is frequently brought into contrast with that of Charlotte Brontë. **George Eliot** was born at Griff in Warwickshire, her real 1819-1880 name being Mary Ann Evans. She was for a time at a school at Nuneaton, and afterwards at Coventry. At first she was an evangelical church-woman, but about 1842 she became acquainted with two or three cultivated women friends at whose houses she met Froude, Emerson, and Francis Newman, all of whom represented a reverent antagonism to supernatural Christianity. In conjunction with Sarah Hennell, she undertook a translation of Strauss's "Life of Jesus." On her father's death, in 1849, she came to London and became associated with Dr Chapman in the editorship of the *Westminster Review*. It was her friendship with George Henry Lewes, whom she met in 1851, which gave her the first impulse towards fiction. Lewes was an active critic, and a writer of two now forgotten novels. Miss Evans's "Scenes of Clerical Life" were sent to Blackwood's Magazine in 1856. The stories were a great success. Thackeray and Dickens were loud in expressions of admiration. In 1859 "Adam Bede" was published and made George Eliot famous. "It is the finest thing since Shakspere," said Charles Reade. Her success, however, did not lead to hasty production. She wrote only six novels during the remainder of her life. "I can write no word that is not prompted from within," she said. "The Mill on the Floss" was written in 1860; "Silas Marner" in 1861; "Romola" in 1863; "Felix Holt" in 1866; "Middlemarch" in 1871-1872; and "Daniel Deronda" in 1876.

In 1880 Miss Mary Ann Evans became Mrs Walter Cross, but after a few months of wedded life she died of inflammation of the heart at 4 Cheyne Walk, Chelsea. Her husband wrote her biography, not with much success. So entirely was George Eliot's best mind concentrated upon her books that her letters, and indeed her personality, were a disappointment to all but a few hero-worshippers.

The novels, with two volumes of poems and two of essays, make up George Eliot's collected works. The essays written before and after her novels give, like her letters, but few indications of her remarkable powers. Nor, although "The Spanish Gipsy" is deeply interesting, can her poetry be counted for much. "The Choir Invisible" is her best known poem. It is by her novels that she must be judged, and these, for insight into character, analysis of the motives which guide men, and sympathy with the intellectual and moral struggles which make up so large a part of life, have a literary niche to themselves. With singular catholicity she paints the simplest faith and the highest idealism. Whether it be an Evangelical clergyman, a Dissenting minister, or a Methodist factory-girl, she enters into the spirit of their lives with fullest sympathy. Carlyle could see in Methodism only "a religion fit for gross and vulgar-minded people, a religion so-called, and the essence of it *cowardice* and *hunger*, terror of pain and appetite for pleasure both carried to the infinite." George Eliot's sympathies were wider. She won the heart of Methodists, who have stood in imagination listening to Dinah Morris addressing the Hayslope peasantry, as she gained the devotion of Roman Catholics like Lord Acton, who have seen in her portrait of Savonarola a wise expression of their faith. And it is not only in religious matters that her sympathies are so broad. The sententious dulness of Mr Macey is as much within the range of her feelings as the manliness of Adam Bede or the scholastic pride of old Bardo. She feels equally for the weak and frivolous Hetty and the lofty, self-sustained Romola. "At least eighty out of a hundred," she says, "of your adult male fellow - Britons returned in the last census are neither extraordinarily silly nor extraordinarily wicked, nor extraordinarily wise; their eyes are neither deep and liquid with sentiment, nor sparkling with suppressed witticisms; they have probably had no hairbreadth escapes or thrilling adventures; their brains are certainly not pregnant with genius, and their passions have not manifested themselves at all after the fashion of a volcano. They are simply men of complexions more or less muddy, whose conversation is more or less bald and disjointed. Yet these commonplace people— many of them—bear a conscience, and have felt the sublime promptings to do the painful right; they have their unspoken sorrows and their sacred joys; their hearts have perhaps gone out towards their first-born, and they have mourned over the irreclaimable dead. Nay, is there not a pathos in their very insignificance, in our comparison of their dim and narrow existence with the glorious possibilities of that human nature which they share? Depend upon it you would gain unspeakably if you would learn with me to see some of the poetry and the pathos, the tragedy and the comedy, lying in the experience of a human soul that looks out through dull gray eyes, and that speaks in a voice of quite ordinary tones." The creations of George Eliot,—Tito and Baldassare, Mrs Poyser and Silas Marner, Dorothy Brooke and Gwendolen,— are not as familiar to the reading public of to-day as they were to that of ten or fifteen years ago.

Victorian Literature

Of the idolatry which almost made her a prophetess of a new cult we hear nothing now She has not maintained her position as Dickens, Thackeray, and Charlotte Brontë have maintained theirs. But if there be little of partisanship and much detraction, it is idle to deny that George Eliot's many gifts, her humour, her pathos, her remarkable intellectual endowments, give her an assured place among the writers of Victorian literature.

The next in order of prominence among the novelists of the period is **Charles Kingsley.** He 1819-1875 was born at Holne Vicarage, on the borders of Dartmoor, and was educated at King's College, London, and Magdalen College, Cambridge. After this he received the curacy of Eversley, in Hampshire, of which parish he finally became rector. In 1848 he published a drama entitled "The Saint's Tragedy," with St Elizabeth of Hungary as heroine. A year later his novel of "Alton Locke" gained him the title of "The Chartist Parson." This tale, in which Carlyle is introduced in the person of an old Scotch bookseller, was a crude and yet vigorous expression of sympathy with the Chartist movement, and its influence was tremendous. For its sympathy with the working classes, and in its reflection of the broad and tolerant Christianity of which Kingsley was always the eloquent preacher, " Alton Locke," in common with " Yeast " and " Two Years Ago," is a valuable contribution to literature. Kingsley, however, became a truer artist when, as in " Hypatia " and " Westward Ho ! " he had not social and religious ends in view. " Hypatia," in spite of many historical errors, is a brilliant sketch of the early Church at Alexandria. Gibbon, from whom Kingsley obtained the hint for this book, would have revelled in the apparent endorsement by a latter-day clergyman of his estimate of the early Christianity of the East. " Westward Ho ! " is a picturesque narrative of English rivalry with Spain in the reign of Elizabeth. The contrasts of character in Frank and Amyas Leigh perhaps give this novel a claim to be considered Kingsley's best effort. He wrote many other works, including children's stories, scientific lectures, and poems, among which last the beautiful ballads, " The Three Fishers " and " The Sands of Dee," are the most popular. For nine years he held the office of Professor of Modern History at Cambridge University, but his unphilosophical views of history made his presence there a misfortune. A model country clergyman, a man essentially healthy-minded and interested in all phases of life and thought, Kingsley's influence, especially on young men, during the past five-

and-thirty years, has been very great and very beneficial.

Henry Kingsley, a younger brother of Charles, 1830-1876 wrote many novels and romances, three of them memorable. " Geoffrey Hamlyn" is popular as the best novel of Australian life. To Australia he had gone to make his fortune at the diggings. He did not make a fortune, but joined the colonial mounted police instead. Compelled by his office to attend an execution, he threw up the post in disgust, and returned to England to find his brother installed as Vicar of Eversley and on the high road to fame. Little wonder that he attempted to emulate him, and he succeeded.

Never, surely, has literature produced two brothers so remarkable, and at the same time so different. Both gave us energetic heroes, and loved manliness. In Charles Kingsley, however, the novelist was always largely subordinated to the preacher. In Henry there was nothing of the preacher whatever. " Geoffrey Hamlyn," " Ravenshoe" and "The Hillyars and The Burtons," are all forcible, effective works, and they have secured generous praise and appreciation from many a literary colleague. But Henry was a bit of a ne'er-do-well, and so his personality has been carefully screened from the public. His name is not even mentioned in Charles Kingsley's biography. Sir Edwin Arnold, however, who knew him at Oxford, and Mrs Thackeray Ritchie, who knew him towards the end of his life, testify to certain delightful qualities of mind and heart which peculiarly appealed to them.[1]

A writer not less successful than Charles Kingsley, but in no way comparable as a man, 1803-1873 was **Edward Bulwer Lytton**, Baron Lytton, who was born in London, and created no small sensation in 1828 by the publication of "Pelham." This was followed by a long list of novels of infinite variety. Some dealt with the preternatural like "Zanoni," and others with history, psychology, and ethics. Of these the most popular were doubtless the historical "Harold," "Rienzi," "The Last of the Barons," and "The Last Days of Pompeii," which still hold their own with the younger generation. The thoughtful men of to-day do not however read "The Caxtons" as they did in the sixties and seventies. Lytton was one of the cleverest men of his age—using the word in no friendly sense—he was a clever novelist, a clever dramatist (his comedy of "Money," and his tragedies "Richelieu" and "The Lady of Lyons," still

[1] Charles Kingsley's novels and miscellaneous writings are published by Macmillan & Co., in twenty-nine volumes. Henry Kingsley's novels have been recently issued by Ward & Lock in twelve volumes.

hold the stage), and a clever Parliamentary debater.

Another writer, with higher claims to consideration than those of literature, was **Benjamin Disraeli, 1804-1881** Earl of Beaconsfield. Disraeli entered life under conditions peculiarly favourable to a successful literary career. His father, Isaac D'Israeli, was an enthusiastic bookworm, whose " Curiosities of Literature " and other books are an inexhaustible mine of anecdote on the quarrels and calamities of authors. The young Disraeli wrote " Vivian Grey " in 1827, following this very successful effort with " The Young Duke," " Venetia," " Henrietta Temple," and other novels. In 1837 he was returned to Parliament as member for Maidstone. His career as an orator and statesman does not concern us here ; suffice to say that of his many later novels " Coningsby," " Tancred," and " Sybil " are by far the ablest and most brilliant, and that " Sybil " was an effective exposure of many abuses in the relations of capital to labour. In addition to his work as a novelist, Lord Beaconsfield wrote an able biography of his friend and colleague, Lord George Bentinck.

One of the most successful of the greater novelists of the reign was **Charles Reade**, who first 1814-1884 became famous by "Peg Woffington" in 1852. "The Cloister and the Hearth" was published in 1861, and "Griffith Gaunt" in 1866. Several of his later novels were written "with a purpose." In "Hard Cash" he drew attention to the abuses of private lunatic asylums; in "Foul Play" he aroused public interest in the iniquities of ship-knackers; in "Put Yourself in His Place," he attacked Trades Unions, and in "Never Too Late to Mend" he exposed some of the abuses of our prison system as it existed at that time. Reade was also an industrious dramatist; "Masks and Faces," and "Drink," are among his most popular plays. Of all his books "The Cloister and the Hearth" is the best, and also the most widely read. It has for its hero the father of Erasmus.

Those who in days to come will want to know what provincial life was really like in England in early Victorian times will enquire for the **1815-1882** novels of **Anthony Trollope**. "Barchester Towers," "Framley Parsonage," and "Dr Thorne," are the most popular of a series of tales, in all of which the country life of England, its clergy and squirearchy, are portrayed. Trollope wrote on many subjects. His "Life of Cicero" secured the commendation of Professor Freeman, and his biography of Thackeray, though all too slight, is the best book about

Victorian Literature

the author of "Vanity Fair" that has so far
been given us.

Another novelist of about equal status with
Trollope in mid-Victorian fiction is **George John
Whyte Melville**. Major Whyte Melville is the 1821-1878
novelist of all lovers of the hunting-field, and
strangely enough he fell a victim to the very
sport which he had done so much to picture.
He was killed by a fall from his horse. Whyte
Melville's hunting novels include "Katerfelto"
and "Black but Comely." He also wrote historical
novels, of which "The Queen's Maries" and "The
Gladiators" were the most popular, and he had a
pretty gift of verse.

Literature has rarely produced a more picturesque figure than **Robert Louis Stevenson**. 1850-1894
The son of a famous Scottish engineer he was
destined, like his great countryman Sir Walter
Scott, for a Writership to the Signet. He took,
however, to literature instead, and died at forty-
four in Samoa,—where he had gone for his health,
—after a remarkable literary achievement. With
a style not always rigidly grammatical, but always impressive and distinguished, he shone in
many branches of literary work. He wrote
travel pictures like "With a Donkey in the
Cevennes," which were incomparably superior to
those of any contemporary ; his plays—written

59

in collaboration with Mr W. E. Henley—had a power of their own, and one of them, " Beau Austin," although not accepted by the public, is probably the greatest contribution to the drama of the era. As a critic of life and of books Stevenson has also an honourable place. I know of no better treatment of the one than " Virginibus Puerisque," or of the other than " Some Aspects of Robert Burns." He has given abundant pleasure to children by " A Child's Garden of Verses," and in " Underwoods " he has scarcely less successfully appealed to their elders.

It is as a novelist, however, that Stevenson fills the largest place. He is the inheritor of the traditions of Scott, with the world-pain of his own epoch superadded. Men and boys alike have found " Treasure Island " absorbing, while men have also pondered over the widely different powers which are displayed in " The New Arabian Nights " and " The Master of Ballantrae," " Prince Otto," and " St Ives." " Dr Jekyll and Mr Hyde " is a parable which has thrilled us all.

Stevenson delighted to call Mr George Meredith his master, and the two men were friends of 1828- years. **George Meredith** began his literary career in 1851, with a volume of poems, one of which, " Love in a Valley," is still an unqualified joy to all who read it. Mr Meredith has published

Victorian Literature

several volumes of poems since then, and all of them have their loyal admirers, but it is as a novelist that the world at large appraises him.

His concentrated thought and vivid passion have gained for him the title of the "Browning of novelists." Each of his books in turn has had its ardent partisans among cultivated and thoughtful readers. "The Shaving of Shagpat" appeared in 1856, and "Farina" in 1857. "The Ordeal of Richard Feverel," which appeared in 1859, is by many considered Meredith's best novel. It treats, with subtle humour and profound philosophical insight, of the problem of a youth's education, and is full of truth to life. "Feverel" was followed by "Evan Harrington" (1861), while "Rhoda Fleming" (1865), "The Adventures of Harry Richmond" (1871), "Beauchamp's Career" (1876), "The Egoist" (1879), "The Tragic Comedians" (1881), and "Diana of the Crossways" (1885), have each of them abundance of readers. Merely to enumerate George Meredith's novels is to call to the memory of all who have read them a widening of mental and moral vision. The rich vein of poetry running through the books, their humour and imagination, place their author in the very front rank of English novelists. "I should never forgive myself," said Robert Louis Stevenson, "if I forgot 'The Egoist,' which, of all the novels I have read (and I have read thousands), stands in a place by itself. I have read 'The Egoist' five or six times, and I mean to read it again." Others have spoken with equal enthusiasm of "Sandra Belloni," with its sweet singer Emilia; others of "Beauchamp's Career," with its aristocratic Radical, now generally understood to have been intended for Admiral Maxse.

Mr Meredith dedicated his volume of "Poems" 1785-1866 of 1851 to **Thomas Love Peacock**, who, perhaps, more than any other writer influenced his own style. Peacock was born at Weymouth, and he was mainly self-educated. In 1804 and 1806 he published two small volumes of poetry, "The Monks of St Mark" and "Palmyra." In 1812 he became acquainted with Shelley, and the two were intimate at Great Marlow where Peacock lived in 1815, and later. Peacock's novels "Headlong Hall" (1816-1817), "Melincourt" (1817) and "Nightmare Abbey" (1818), which have been two or three times reprinted within the last five or six years, gained no commensurate attention on their appearance, although one of them was translated into French. In 1819 Peacock became a clerk in the India House, and married a Welsh girl, Jane Gryffdh. "Maid Marion" appeared in 1822, "Crotchet Castle" in 1831, and in 1837 "Paper Money Lyrics and other Poems." All the novels I have named, and they are his most famous, belong to the pre-Victorian period, but "Gryll Grange," his last novel, was published in 1861. Peacock is interesting as a novelist and for his relations with other famous men. He was, as I have said, the friend of Shelley, and he was the father-in-law of Mr George Meredith. Added to this he succeeded to James Mill's post at the India House, and vacated it for James Mill's son, John Stuart Mill.

To R. L. Stevenson we undoubtedly owe much of the impulse to the modern romantic movement, which adds every day an historical novel or a story of adventure to our libraries. It has given us Stanley Weyman, "Q" (A. T. Quiller Couch), "Anthony Hope," Max Pemberton, and Conan Doyle, the creator of Sherlock Holmes. Another Scotsman, George MacDonald, whose "Robert Falconer," 1824-"David Elginbrod," and "Alec Forbes of Howglen," have charmed nearly a generation, had less influence than might have been thought upon the younger Scottish writers, who have made Scottish scenes and Scottish dialect so marked an element in many popular works. James Matthew Barrie, for example, had written "A Window in Thrums," before he had read one of Dr Mac-Donald's books. Mr Barrie was probably influenced, however, by John Galt (1779-1859), whose "Ayrshire Legatees" and "Annals of the

Parish" were written before the Queen began to reign.

A writer whose most striking book was published sufficiently long ago to justify its inclusion here, was **Joseph Henry Shorthouse.** His "John Inglesant" gained for him a reputation which his "Sir Percival" did not sustain. Mr Shorthouse has written nothing since "John Inglesant" so beautiful as his "Little Schoolmaster Mark," a singularly poetical conception of abnormal childhood.

1834-

The best stories for children have been written by **Lewis Carroll.** This is the pseudonym of the Rev. Charles Lutwidge Dodgson, a lecturer on mathematics at Christ Church, Oxford, and the author of several mathematical text-books. In "Euclid and his Modern Rivals" and "A Tangled Tale," Mr Dodgson has succeeded in combining his taste for science with a rich humour, but his fame rests upon his remarkable fairy-stories, "Alice's Adventures in Wonderland," published in 1865, and its sequel, "Through the Looking-Glass," which appeared in 1872. Men and women, quite as much as little children, have found pleasure and entertainment in these happy efforts of a genius as individual as anything our age has produced.

1833-

I have purposely all but ignored many writers of fiction who are still actively engaged in literary pursuits. The daily journals bring their achievements sufficiently to the front. But literary workers owe so much to the untiring zeal of **Sir Walter Besant** in their behalf, that at the risk of 1838- inconsistency, I mention his "All Sorts and Conditions of Men," a story which not only sold by thousands, but had a practical influence such as is rarely given to poet or novelist to achieve. The writer dreams of a wealthy heiress devoting her time and money to purifying and elevating the East End of London. She builds a Palace of Delight, and devotes it to the service of the people. In May, 1887, the dream was realised, for the Queen opened just such a Palace for the People in the Mile-End Road. How far this institution, the outcome of a novelist's imagination and the generous subscriptions of philanthropists, has achieved the regeneration of the London poor, history has yet to record. Sir Walter Besant wrote at an earlier period twelve novels in conjunction with **James Rice**, a collaborator of singular 1843-1882 humour and imagination. Of the books written conjointly, "Ready Money Mortiboy" and "The Golden Butterfly" are the most popular.

Passing from the acknowledged masters in imaginative literature, one turns to a crowd of popular and interesting writers who have charmed and delighted multitudes of readers. Foremost

among these are Lever and Marryat. **Charles**
1806-1872 **Lever** was for some time editor of the *Dublin
University Magazine*, but his Irish stories,
" Charles O'Malley " and " Harry Lorrequer "
are his chief title to fame. That the rollicking
humour of these books still commands attention
is proved by a recent luxurious re-issue of them.[1]

Another Irishman, who won the affections of
Irishmen as Lever won their laughter, was **William**
1798-1869 **Carleton,** who was born at Prillisk, county Tyrone.
He was the youngest of fourteen children. His
equal knowledge of Irish and English gave him an
intimacy with the folk-lore and fairy tales, which
make up so large a part in the lives of the poorer
among his countrymen, and " Traits and Stories
of the Irish Peasantry " (1833) and " Tales of
Ireland " (1834), were the result. His romance,
" Fardorougha the Miser," appeared in 1839, and
he treated in 1847 of the horrors of the Irish
famine in his " Black Prophet." Carleton has
for many years ceased to be read in England,
but he shares in the revived interest in Irish
literature, which has taken the place of interest
1814-1873 in Irish politics. **Joseph Sheridan Le Fanu** also
made a great success with " Uncle Silas " (1864)
and " In a Glass Darkly " (1872).

1792-1848 **Frederick Marryat** ran away to sea several

[1] " The Collected Works of Charles Lever." Downey
& Co.

times before his father, a member of Parliament of
great wealth, consented to his being a sailor. He
was a successful and popular naval officer before
he was twenty-one. He was thirty-seven years
of age when he wrote his first novel, "Frank
Mildmay," the success of which led him to adopt
literature as the profession of his later life. Of
his many novels, of which "Mr Midshipman Easy"
and "Peter Simple" are perhaps the best, several
appeared in the *Metropolitan Magazine*, which
Marryat edited for four years. Not only is
Marryat the most delightful of writers for boys,
but it is interesting to note that both Carlyle
and Ruskin during long terms of illness solaced
themselves with his wonderful sea-stories.

A writer who gave much healthy pleasure
to schoolboys was **William Henry Giles King-** 1814-1880
ston, who left behind him one hundred and
twenty-five stories of the sea. Another writer
for boys, **William Harrison Ainsworth,** was the 1805-1882
son of a Manchester solicitor. The majority of
his thirty novels treat of historical themes. The
best of them, "Old St Paul's," "The Tower of
London," and "Rookwood," have been translated into most modern languages. Scarcely less
popular for a time was **G. P. R. James,** who also 1801-1860
dealt freely with history. Thackeray burlesqued
James so skilfully that he has already become

a tradition. He was British Consul in Virginia, and afterwards at Venice, where he died.

Living English novelists of well-deserved popularity, are Mr Hardy, Mr Black, and Mr Blackmore.

1840- **Thomas Hardy** made his earlier fame by "Far from the Madding Crowd" (1874). He made his later popularity by "Tess of the D'Urbervilles" (1892). Between these books came two stories greater than either—"The Return of the Native" (1878) and "The Woodlanders" (1887). One must read those books to appreciate how very great a novelist Mr Hardy is, how full of poetry and of insight. The Dorsetshire landscape which, under the guise of "Wessex," he has made so familiar, will be classic ground for many a day to all lovers of good literature.

1841- Although **William Black**, who was born in Glasgow, has written numerous stories about the West Highlands of Scotland, he has no affinity whatever to the new Scotch school. He made his first appearance as a novelist in 1867 with "Love or Marriage," and almost every year since he has published a story, over thirty novels now bearing his name. Black has recognised the value of the picturesque back-ground afforded by West Highland scenery, with its accompanying incidents in the outdoor life of the deer stalker and angler. He has given us some real characterization in

Victorian Literature

"A Daughter of Heth" (1871), in "Madcap Violet" (1876): while "Macleod of Dare" (1878) is perhaps the best thing he has written.

Richard Doddridge Blackmore has written many interesting novels, but it has been his perverse fate to live by only one of them. "Lorna Doone" was published in 1869, and although received coldly at first, finally achieved great popularity: and visits to the Lorna Doone country, as that part of Devonshire is called, make part of the travelled education of every literary American. As a master of rustic comedy he stands unexcelled in our day, and the merits of certain other novels—"The Maid of Sker," "Christowell" and "Cripps the Carrier"— may some day become more fully recognised. **1825-**

Not less popular than the novelist of locality— for this description may surely be applied to Mr Hardy and the two other writers I have named—is the novelist of sensation. **William Wilkie Collins** was the most prominent exponent of that School. **1824-1889** "The Woman in White," which appeared in 1860 in *All the Year Round*, took the town by storm, but Count Fosco would be pronounced a tiresome villain to-day. With "The Moonstone" and "The New Magdalen" Wilkie Collins secured almost equal success. Although it has been affirmed that a new Wilkie Collins, that is to say a novelist of pure

69

sensation, might even now have a great vogue, it is quite certain that the actual Wilkie Collins has lost the greater part of his.[1] Another novelist who presents himself as little more than a name to the **1807-1877** present generation is **Samuel Warren**. He was a doctor, and, like his homotype, Mr Conan Doyle half a century later, studied medicine at the University of Edinburgh. His "Passages from the Diary of a Late Physician" began in *Blackwood's Magazine* in 1830, and was well received, but a still greater success attended his "Ten Thousand a Year," which appeared first in the same periodical.

Time has dealt unkindly with Samuel Warren: it is yet to be seen how time will deal with another **1820-1887** popular favourite, **Mrs Henry Wood**, who was born in Worcestershire and made the city of Worcester the centre of many of her stories. The "Channings" and "Mrs Halliburton's Troubles" are her best novels and they have had a well-deserved popularity, for Mrs Wood had a splendid faculty for telling a story. Her even more popular novel, "East Lynne," will probably survive for many a year as a stage play.

Next to Charlotte Brontë and George Eliot the

[1] A New Library Edition of the novels of Wilkie Collins has just been published by Chatto and Windus.

most distinguished woman novelist of the era is
Mrs Gaskell, who, as Elizabeth Cleghorn Stevenson, 1810-1865
married William Gaskell, a Unitarian minister of
Manchester. Mrs Gaskell's first literary success
was "Mary Barton," the story of a Manchester
factory girl. "Ruth," "North and South," and
"Sylvia's Lovers" were equally successful, but the
two books which are certain to secure immortality
to their author are "Cranford" (1853), and "The
Life of Charlotte Brontë" (1857). "Cranford"
is an idyll of village life which is sure to charm
many generations of readers, and not a few artists
have delighted to illustrate its quaint and fascinating character studies. "Cranford" has been iden-
tified with Knutsford in Cheshire. Mrs Gaskell's
biography of her friend Charlotte Brontë has
probably had a larger sale than any other biography in our literature. Many causes contributed
to this—the popularity of the Brontë novels, the
exceptionally romantic and pathetic life of their
authors, Mrs Gaskell's own fame as a writer of
fiction, and the literary skill with which she treated
the material at her command.

Other women writers who have had a large
measure of fame, and are now well-nigh forgotten,
are Mrs Marsh (1791-1874), who wrote "The
Admiral's Daughter" and "The Deformed," Mrs
Crowe (1800-1876), who wrote "Susan Hopley"

and "The Night Side of Nature," Mrs Archer
Clive (1801-1873), who wrote "Paul Ferroll,"
Lady Georgiana Fullerton (1812-1885), the author
of "Ann Sherwood," Mrs Stretton (1812-1878),
who wrote "The Valley of a Hundred Fires."

All these are now little more than names to us,
1800-1879 but not so **Anne Manning**, whose "Maiden and
Married Life of Mary Powell" will long continue to
be read. It is an effective presentation of Milton
1808-1877 and his first wife. **Mrs Norton,** "the Byron of
poetesses," as Lockhart described her, wrote several
novels, "Stuart of Dunleath" and "Lost and
Saved" being perhaps the best known in their time,
but she lives now mainly in George Meredith's
1826-1887 "Diana of the Crossways." **Dinah Mulock** (Mrs
Craik) may still be ranked among our most popular
novelists, although her best and most successful
book "John Halifax, Gentleman," was published
1824-1877 in 1857. The memory of **Julia Kavanagh,** although her "Madeleine" was enthusiastically
greeted on its appearance, has all but faded
away. Miss Kavanagh's "Woman in France in
the 18th Century," "English Women of Letters,"
and "French Women of Letters," were handsomely
got-up books, and are still to be found in many
old-fashioned libraries.

Two of the most popular writers for children

Victorian Literature

were A. L. O. E. and Mrs Ewing. A. L. O. E.
or A Lady of England, was the pseudonym of
Charlotte Maria Tucker, who after many years of 1821-1893
successful literary labour, went out to India for
the Church Missionary Society, at the age of fifty-
four. Miss Tucker's most popular stories were
"Pride and his Pursuers," "Exiles in Babylon,"
"House Beautiful," and "Cyril Ashley." Scarcely
less popular was **Mrs Ewing,** whose mother, Mrs 1841-1885
Gatty, edited *Aunt Judy's Magazine.* It was in
this magazine that Mrs Ewing's "Remembrances
of Mrs Overtheway" made their appearance.

Another writer of great popularity, **Mrs Charles,** 1828-1896
secured an immense success with "The Schönberg-
Cotta Family," "Kitty Trevelyan's Diary," and
other books of a semi-religious, semi-historical
tendency. It is a natural association, not derived
from similarity of name, to mention **Maria Louisa**
Charlesworth at the same time, because Miss 1819-1880
Charlesworth's "Ministering Children" had an
enormous success with the religious public of
England,—the public which supports Missionary
Societies and Sunday Schools.

I might easily devote many pages to the living
women novelists who have impressed themselves
upon the era; but that scarcely comes within the
scope of this little book. There are, to name but

a few, Mrs Lynn Linton, Mrs Humphry Ward, Ouida, Miss Braddon, Miss Marie Corelli, Miss Olive Schreiner, Miss Rhoda Broughton, Edna Lyall, Lucas Malet, Miss Charlotte Yonge, Miss Adeline Sergeant, Mrs Macquoid, Mrs Alexander, Mrs W. K. Clifford—names which recall to thousands of readers many familiar books and some of the happiest hours they have ever spent.

1828-1897 With the name of **Mrs Oliphant**, who has recently died, I may fitly close this survey of Victorian fiction. Mrs Oliphant struck the note of the era alike in her versatility and in her lack of thoroughness. She was so versatile that she once offered to write a whole number of *Blackwood's Magazine*, a publication to which she was for years a valued contributor. And she would have done it with fair effectiveness. That she wrote good fiction is now generally acknowledged. She wrote also biography, criticism, and every form of prose. Her "Makers of Florence" has been a popular history,—it treats of Dante, Giotto, and Savonarola,—as her "Life of Edward Irving" has been a popular biography. She wrote many other books apart from her fiction, "A History of Eighteenth Century Literature," a "Memoir of Principal Tulloch," biographies of Cervantes and Molière, and a volume on "Dress." But she was not a good critic, nor was she a very accurate

Victorian Literature

student. It is upon her novels that her fame will have to rest. "Salem Chapel," a skilful delineation of a minister and his congregation, has been compared to George Eliot's "Silas Marner." "Passages in the Life of Margaret Maitland" (1849) was her first novel and "The Lady's Walk" (1897) her last, and in the intervening years she probably wrote sixty or seventy stories, each of them containing indications of a genius which, with more concentration, would have given her an enduring place in English fiction.

CHAPTER III

The Historians

THE reign of Victoria has been pre-eminently the reign of the historian in our literature. Greater poets we had seen in the reigns of the Georges, greater essayists in the reign of Anne. But Grote and Carlyle, Macaulay and Gardiner, Bishop Stubbs and Dr Freeman, had no counterparts in an earlier age—always excepting the one great name of Gibbon. Before them there were chroniclers of contemporary events and pamphleteers under the guise of historians, but little more. Goldsmith's histories are the laughing - stock of those to whom the modern methods of research are familiar, and even Hume had little of the spirit of the genuine student. Hallam and Lingard were the pioneers in this branch of literature, although both of them had done their work before Queen Victoria came to the throne.

Henry Hallam was born at Windsor, where his 1777-1859 father held a canonry. His first great work, entitled "View of the State of Europe during the

77

Middle Ages," was published in 1818, and his "Constitutional History of England, from the Accession of Henry VII. to the Death of George II.," in 1827. In 1838 he produced his "Introduction to the Literature of Europe in the Fifteenth, Sixteenth, and Seventeenth Centuries." Of these three works the first and the last are valuable mainly for their stimulus to the more philosophical and imaginative work of later writers, but the "Constitutional History" remains the text-book for the period which it covers. Macaulay praised it highly, possibly because of the Whiggism which undoubtedly underlies some of the more debatable propositions in the book; but Macaulay and many other writers have disputed the correctness of many of Hallam's judgments. To write the constitutional history of England from the earliest period to the year 1485, where Hallam begins, was a far more difficult undertaking than to deal with the reigns of the Tudors and the Stuarts. This work devolved on Dr Stubbs.

1825-   **William Stubbs**, who was appointed Bishop of Oxford in 1889, was born at Knaresborough, and was educated at Ripon Grammar School and at Christ Church, Oxford. In 1850 he became vicar of Navestock, in Essex, and in 1862 he was made librarian at Lambeth Palace. His editions of mediæval chronicles were well calculated to smooth the path of any future historian, and the critical

Victorian Literature

introductions showed the profound scholarship of
the editor. Probably no one man has done so
much to throw light on the obscure by-ways of
history, and as Regius Professor of Modern History at Oxford, a post he accepted in 1866, he
gave so great a stimulus to historical study that
many brilliant writers have since been proud to
call him "master." In 1870 he published his
"Select Charters," of which the "Introductions"
are also invaluable, and between 1874 and 1878
he wrote his great work, "The Constitutional
History of England in its Origin and Development," the three volumes of which carry us down
to the death of Richard III. The book is profoundly scientific in its method, but it is a mis-
taken, although popular, belief which classes Dr
Stubbs among Dryasdust investigators. The work
glows with life and interest, and is full of suggestive
parallels for modern political society.

The work of tracing the growth of the English
constitution, which had been so worthily begun by
Hallam, and continued in so wise and scholarly a
fashion by Bishop Stubbs, was carried on by **Sir
Thomas Erskine May,** who, a few days before his **1815-1886**
death, was created Baron Farnborough. After a
long official career in connection with the House
of Commons, he was appointed Clerk to the House
in 1871. In addition to several publications dealing with Parliamentary forms, and a book on

"Democracy in Europe," he wrote a "Constitutional History since the Accession of George III.," thus continuing the work from the point at which Hallam had dropped it, and completing a continuous history of the English Constitution.

When we turn to what is more popularly understood by the history of a country, the political and social life of peoples, and the wars and conquests of nations, we are not less fortunate in the results 1771-1851 attained. **John Lingard** had, it is true, written his great work before 1837. "The History of England, from the First Invasion by the Romans to the Commencement of the Reign of William III.," appeared in eight volumes between 1819 and 1830. Lingard was the son of a Winchester carpenter. He was for some time the Professor of Moral Philosophy at a Roman Catholic College. His religious views doubtless affected, in considerable measure, his judgment of events, especially in the reign of Henry VIII., but he is a fairly impartial historian. He confesses that he has been more anxious to arrive at the facts than troubled as to the garb in which those facts were presented to the public, and his work is really very dull in consequence. A contemporary of Lingard, who covered much of the same historic ground, was Sharon Turner, (1768-1847), and yet another was 1807-1857 **John Mitchell Kemble**, whose "Saxons in England" (1849) still fills a useful place. Another distinguished writer, of what we may term the earlier school of historical research, was **Sir Francis Palgrave**, one of whose accomplished sons, Francis **1788-1861** Turner Palgrave, is still living (born 1824), whilom Professor of Poetry at Oxford and the friend of Tennyson, the author of excellent verse, and, moreover, the editor of that incomparable volume, the "Golden Treasury of Songs and Lyrics." Sir Francis was the son of a Jewish stockbroker named Cohen, and changed his name on becoming a Christian. His best book, the " History of Normandy and of England," lost much of its value by the publication of Freeman's monumental work, " The History of the Norman Conquest."

Edward Augustus Freeman was born at Har- **1823-1892** borne, in Staffordshire, and educated at Trinity College, Oxford. His first work was a " History of Architecture," published in 1849. In 1863 he issued the first volume of a "History of Federal Government." The "History of the Norman Conquest," in five large volumes, appeared between 1867 and 1876, and the "Reign of William Rufus, and Accession of Henry I.," in 1882. His "Old English History" was a most delightful collection of the primitive stories which have always had a great fascination for beginners in history. There was scarcely any period of European history with which the author of the "Norman

Conquest" did not show a thorough familiarity. No historian has had a keener grasp of hard solid facts, or is more able to make common-sense deductions from them. " I am quite unable," he candidly confessed, " to appreciate physical or metaphysical works in any language," and he hated literary discussion, which he contemptuously termed " Chatter about Harriet," in reference to the debatable question of Shelley's treatment of his wife. Perhaps this lack of breadth did not materially spoil him for his work. Of his many volumes of histories and essays, those on the " Norman Conquest" must be given the first place. It has been said, indeed, that the work takes as long to read as the event took to achieve, but it is worth reading nevertheless. The battle of Hastings, or, as Mr Freeman would say, of Senlac, was a turning-point in our national history, and we have here the most complete description of that great struggle. Since Freeman's death some attempt has been made to question his accuracy and his scholarship; but it has not amounted to very much. When Dr Stubbs, with whom difference of political views has in no way impaired a lifelong friendship, was appointed Bishop of Chester in 1884, Mr Freeman succeeded him as Regius Professor of Modern History at Oxford, where he was followed on his death by Mr Froude.

Victorian Literature

It would be hard to find a greater contrast, both in method and in manner, than between Edward Freeman and James Anthony Froude. Freeman's style, though clear and trenchant, was never brilliant; Froude's language compares with that of the best artists in literature. Freeman was always scrupulously exact, never at fault in a fact or a date; Froude was notoriously careless, and slipped at every turn. Freeman cared nothing for theories; Froude was never so happy as when he stopped abruptly in a description to discourse on the mysteries of Providence or the follies of mankind. Between men of such opposite natures no friendship was possible, and in the *Saturday Review* and other periodicals Freeman commented vigorously, and not always fairly, on the other's inaccuracy.

James Anthony Froude was one of three gifted 1818-1894 brothers, another being William Froude (1810-1879), the mathematician and engineer; and the third, Richard Hurrell Froude (1803-1836), a leader of the Tractarian movement, whose " Literary Remains " were published after his death by Keble and Newman. Froude was educated at Oriel College, Oxford, and for a time came under the influence of the movement of which his elder brother was a leading spirit, but ultimately he abandoned supernatural Christianity altogether, substituting for it a kind of

poetic Theism which he partly adopted from
Carlyle. In 1847 he published anonymously two
novels, "The Spirit's Trials" and "The Lieutenant's
Daughter," which contained some not very generous
criticisms on his brother and former friends. His
"Nemesis of Faith," which appeared in 1848, was
a further criticism of the doctrines which he had
abandoned. Between the years 1856 and 1869 he
published the twelve volumes of his great work,
"The History of England, from the Fall of Wolsey
to the Defeat of the Spanish Armada," which
achieved a great and, in many respects, a well-
deserved popularity. Rarely indeed has history
been written with so much brilliancy and picturesque power. The earlier volumes have been much
discredited among historical students : yet we would
not willingly miss such delightful word-painting as
his description of the Pilgrimage of Grace and
other scenes in the career of the Eighth Henry,
whom he selected for rehabilitation. It was, of
course, a vain and impossible task to remove the
odium which has settled upon the name of
Henry VIII. ; but it was as well that the attempt
should be made. Henry had appeared to the
mass of modern Englishmen as an old-world ogre,
and Mr Froude has at least enabled them to see
that he was after all a man. Mr Freeman, himself
the most conscientious and laborious of writers,
expressed his hearty contempt for an author who

professed in the preface to his history that he took up the subject because he had "nothing better to do." As, however, Froude warmed to his work his book increased in value, and there are few who will deny the most sterling worth to his "Edward VI.," "Mary," and "Elizabeth." His escape from Tractarianism had made him unfriendly to all kindred movements, and his views of the struggle between Catholicism and Evangelicalism in the sixteenth century are more worthy of a Puritan divine than of an academic writer of our own day. But we can forgive all this, and much more, to one who has described with so much delicate fancy the adventurous life of Drake and Hawkins, the intrigues of the Scottish Queen, and the restless fickleness and untruthfulness of Elizabeth. His exquisite literary style and general breadth of sympathy are shown in such passages as his sketch of the rise of Protestantism and the execution of More and Fisher :—

"Whilst we exult in that chivalry with which the Smithfield martyrs bought England's freedom with their blood, so we will not refuse our admiration to those other gallant men whose high forms, in the sunset of the old faith, stand transfigured on the horizon, tinged with the light of its dying glory."[1]

Inaccuracy and tactlessness, however, seemed to haunt Mr Froude like evil spirits. He wrote a

[1] Froude's "History of England," vol. ii. chap. ix.

series of articles on Thomas à Becket, but the numerous mistakes and misstatements brought down on him once again the strictures of Mr Freeman. He wrote a biography of Carlyle, to whom he acted as literary executor, and the whole of the literary world was in arms at the revelations of Carlyle's somewhat unamiable relations with his wife, and of his too contemptuous sentiments about many personal friends. Still, Mr Froude's great literary faculty will secure to this biography a far greater permanence than will fall to the lot of the thousand-and-one memoirs which have appeared during the reign. Even should Carlyle's writings cease to be generally studied, it is not improbable that Froude's "Life of Carlyle" will always be read as an important chapter in literary history. In this connection I cannot do better than quote from an unpublished letter from Sir Fitz James Stephen, Mr Froude's co-executor, to Mr Froude :—

"For about fifteen years I was the intimate friend and constant companion of both you and Mr Carlyle, and never in my life did I see any one man so much devoted to any other as you were to him during the whole of that period of time. The most affectionate son could not have acted better to the most venerated father. You cared for him, soothed him, protected him as a guide might protect a weak old man down a steep and painful path. The admiration you habitually expressed for him both morally and intellectually was unqualified. You never said to me one ill-natured word about him down to this day. It is to me wholly incredible that anything but a severe regard for truth, learnt to a great extent from his teaching, could ever have led you to embody in your portrait of him a delineation of the faults and weaknesses which mixed with his great qualities.

"Of him I will make only one remark in justice to you. He did not use you well. He threw upon you the responsibility of a decision which he ought to have taken himself in a plain, unmistakable way. He considered himself bound to expiate the wrongs which he had done to his wife. If he had done this himself it would have been a courageous thing; but he did not do it himself. He did not even decide for himself that it should be done after his death. If any courage was shown in the matter, it was shown by you, and not by him. You took the responsibility of deciding for him that it ought to be done. You took the odium of doing it, of avowing to the world the faults and weaknesses of one whom you regarded as your teacher and master. In order to present to the world a true picture of him as he really was, you, well knowing what you were about, stepped into a pillory in which you were charged with treachery, violation of confidence, and every imaginable base motive, when you were in fact guilty of no other fault than that of practising Mr Carlyle's great doctrine that men ought to tell the truth."

Mr Froude has other claims to remembrance. In his " Short Studies on Great Subjects," many of them essays written for *Fraser's Magazine*, of which he was for a long time editor, are some very wise and thoughtful papers, particularly one on the Book of Job. His " Life of Bunyan " is characteristic, as is also his " Life of Cæsar." Carlyle taught him hero-worship, and from Carlyle also he learnt the disposition which inspired his powerful book, "The English in Ireland in the Eighteenth Century."

He also wrote two picturesque books of travel, and three volumes of lectures[1] delivered at Oxford during his occupancy of the chair of history, which had been previously held in succession by his two great rivals, Bishop Stubbs and Dr Freeman.

The historian who devoted himself most earnestly to Mr Froude's chief historical period, and whose writings were in some measure a reply to 1810-1879 his, was the **Rev. John Sherren Brewer**, who for many years was Professor of English Literature at King's College, London. Brewer's chief work, a " Calendar of Letters and Papers, Foreign and Domestic, of the Reign of Henry VIII.," comes down, however, to 1530, the year in which Mr Froude's history commences, and thus Brewer

[1] "Lectures on the Council of Trent," "English Seamen in the Sixteenth Century," and " Life and Letters of Erasmus."

stands alone as an authority on Henry's early reign.
A compressed work in one volume, "The Reign
of Henry VIII.," was published after his death.
Mr Froude concludes his narrative at the year
1588, the year of the Spanish Armada, but no
recent writer of mark has treated of the closing
years of Elizabeth's reign in any detail, although
we owe to Major Martin Hume a well-written
study entitled "The Year after the Armada." Major
Hume, who is the best living authority upon this
period, has also written upon "The Courtships of
Queen Elizabeth," and has edited for the Public
Record Office the Calendar of Spanish State
Papers of Elizabeth.

The next great period of English history, that
of the Stuart kings, is dealt with by Professor
Gardiner. **Samuel Rawson Gardiner** was born at **1829-**
Ropley, in Hampshire, and was educated at Winchester and at Christ Church, Oxford. His whole
life has been devoted to the most laborious research in the annals of the reigns of James I.,
Charles I., and the Protectorate of Cromwell.
He has not, like Mr Froude, taken up history as a
pleasant literary recreation, but has given years of un-
remitting labour to the production of each separate
volume. He is now well into the study of the
Protectorate, the first volume of his history of which
appeared in 1894. He has written many minor

books, one dealing with "The Gunpowder Plot," and another with "Cromwell's Place in History." Mr Gardiner will not perhaps be counted a brilliant writer. He gives us none of the fire and eloquence, almost bordering on poetry, which we find so abundantly in Froude; but he has been described by Sir John Seeley as the only historian who has trodden the controversial ground of seventeenth-century English political history with absolute fairness and impartiality. James and Charles, Buckingham and Bristol, Strafford and Pym, stand out in clear and well-defined lineaments. There is no hero-worship to blind us; no flowing rhetoric to atone for insufficient knowledge. We see these men in their weakness and in their strength, neither side monopolising the virtue and the patriotism, but each, on occasion, acting from noble or ignoble motives. It may be urged that too much attention is devoted to the follies of princes and the intrigues of courtiers, and certainly of the inner life of the nation we get all too little in Mr Gardiner's pages: but it may be fairly said that these books are the safest and best of guides to one of the most important and critical periods in our political history. It is impossible to avoid contrasting Mr Gardiner with a far more popular and more brilliant historian, Lord Macaulay, and the contrast is, in some respects, in favour of the former. Mr Gardiner sees that in

Victorian Literature

dealing with the complexities of human motives we
are on very uncertain and delicate ground. We
need to pause step by step to weigh probabilities
and to qualify our every statement, although such
hesitancy and qualification is not conducive to
brilliant writing.

The importance of this rhetorical principle was
fully grasped by **Thomas Babington Macaulay, 1800-1859**
and, accordingly, in his writings a single definite
and distinct motive is seized upon as the guiding
principle of every action, and, by the simple plan
of ignoring complexities in human character, we
are carried along in an easy manner to positive
and undoubting opinions. "I wish," said Lord
Melbourne, "that I were as cock-sure of *anything*
as Tom Macaulay is of everything;" and the
remark hit off an undoubted failing, at least from
the standpoint of sound and trustworthy workmanship. Macaulay, whose father was a distinguished
philanthropist and slavery abolitionist, was born at
Rothley Temple, in Leicestershire. From a private
school he went to Trinity College, Cambridge.
His earliest efforts in literature were articles for
Knight's *Quarterly Magazine*, and contributions
to the *Edinburgh Review*, the first of which, on
"Milton," drew from Lord Jeffrey the remark,
"The more I think the less I can conceive where
you picked up that style." Perhaps Macaulay's

essays have been more popular even than his history. The extraordinary knowledge they display, the discursive familiarity with all poetry and fiction, ancient and modern, and their enthusiastic interest in historical events, make them a kind of education to men whose reading has been slight, or who are beginners in the art of reading—an art at which Macaulay was such an adept. In 1830 Macaulay entered Parliament as member for Calne, and four years later received the post of member of the Indian Council at Calcutta, with a salary of £10,000 a year. He left India in 1838, having rendered great service to that country by assisting to frame the Indian penal code. After his return to England he sat in Parliament for many years as member for Edinburgh, and for a short time held a seat in Lord Melbourne's Cabinet. Some of his speeches in the House were among the most eloquent and successful to which that assembly has listened. In 1849 the first two volumes of his " History of England from the Accession of James II. " were published. The great success of these and the succeeding volumes made him one of the most popular authors of his day. In 1857 Macaulay was made a Peer, but he never spoke in the House of Lords. He died in December 1859, before he had finished the "Reign of William III.," and was buried in Westminster Abbey. During the later years of

Victorian Literature

Macaulay's life, and for many years after his death, he received the unstinted praise, not only of the great mass of readers, but even of cultured brother authors. Of late years this has changed; a reaction has set in, and perhaps the time has not yet come to assign to him his true place in literature. When Sir George Trevelyan's admirable life of his uncle appeared in 1876, a number of eminent writers based upon that book a criticism of Macaulay's work. Mr Gladstone wrote in the *Quarterly Review*, Mr Leslie Stephen in the *Cornhill Magazine*, and Mr John Morley in the *Fortnightly Review*. In each separate case the review was unfavourable. All alike agreed as to his high qualities as a man; his sincerity, generosity, kindliness, and purity, his love of children and his brotherly devotion ; but each in turn found matter for censure in his work. One condemned his style, another his Whig partialities, another his boundless optimism, and another his errors of judgment or alleged misstatements of facts. It is true that Macaulay is sometimes inaccurate, that he is not seldom unjust to the characters whom he paints so vividly. It is now a commonplace to say that his history was written, as Carlyle said, "to prove that Providence was on the side of the Whigs." It is clear that he was a man of strong literary prejudices, and he undoubtedly owes much of his popularity to the fact that he expresses in grandly rhetorical language the average sentiment of his day, its belief in material prosperity, and its delight in being told that there has been no age of the world so happy as our own. All this is true, and yet it is also true that Macaulay's real services to literature are lost sight of when such an estimate is propounded too harshly.

In spite of obvious deficiencies, Macaulay's history is a great work. It fills up a gap in historical literature, and such incidents as the trial of the seven bishops and the siege of Londonderry excel both in picturesqueness and in accuracy. But Macaulay has claims far beyond his merits as a historian. The critics who condemn him so freely seem to have forgotten their own early years. "If I am in the wrong," said Macaulay of his history, "I shall at least have set the minds of others at work." He has set the minds of others at work. What cultivated man or woman lives, with whom Macaulay's writings have not been among the first books read, who has not been made to feel that all the great poetry, and fiction, and history to which he alludes so freely must be well worth careful study? What matter if in after-years we discover that Macaulay was unjust to Bacon the man, and was entirely ignorant of Bacon the philosopher; or understand clearly what he meant by saying that such critiques as Lessing's " Laocoon " " filled him with wonder and

Victorian Literature

despair?" If we have been encouraged by him to
desire a wider knowledge, if we have learnt from
him to admire so many great writers, so many
famous statesmen, we may surely forgive him
much, if indeed there be anything to forgive.

Earl Stanhope, who did most of his historical 1805-1875
work when, as an expectant peer, he was known as
Lord Mahon, was a great friend of Macaulay's. In
1870 he published a "History of the Reign of
Queen Anne," which began at the year 1701,
and thus served as a connecting link between
Macaulay's history and his own larger work—the
"History of England, from the Peace of Utrecht
down to the Peace of Versailles (1713-1783)."
The continuation of Earl Stanhope's narrative
may be found either in Mr Lecky's "Eighteenth
Century," or in **William Nathaniel Massey's** "His- 1809-1881
tory of England under George III." Mr Massey
brings us down to the Peace of Amiens in 1801,
from which date Harriet Martineau leads us to 1846
in a work ("History of the Peace") which is quite
unworthy of her abilities. The reign of Victoria
has been written by many hands, not the least
successful being the "History of England, 1830-
1873" of the **Rev. William Nassau Molesworth** 1816-1890
of Rochdale, the author also of a "History of the
Church of England." Equally popular is the
"History of Our Own Time, 1830-1897," of **Justin
MacCarthy,** who has also written a "History of 1830-

the Four Georges," and many popular novels. Nor must we forget the brilliant literary effort **1811-1891** of **Alexander William Kinglake** who, in his "History of the War in the Crimea," has made a younger generation familiar with a struggle in which their fathers took so brave a part. Mr Kinglake was for some years the Liberal member for Bridgewater. His first literary effort, "Eothen," a volume of travels, is scarcely less popular than his history. By far the most important work, however, on English history, in a period subsequent to that dealt with by Macaulay, is Lecky's "History of England in the Eighteenth Century," a work of great thoroughness and thoughtfulness, the eighth and concluding volume of which was published in **1838-** 1890. **William Edward Hartpole Lecky**, who was educated at Trinity College, Dublin, which he now represents in Parliament, is one of the most brilliant and suggestive writers of our age. His "Rise and Influence of the Spirit of Rationalism," and "European Morals from Augustus to Charlemagne," as well as the "History of the Eighteenth Century," are justly popular.

It is impossible to enumerate all the important contributions to historical study of the past few years, but the "History of Scotland, from the Invasion of Agricola to the Revolution of 1688," **1809-1881** by **John Hill Burton**, and the "Life and Reign of Richard III.," by James Gairdner must not be

Victorian Literature

forgotten, nor the "History of the War in the Peninsula," by Sir Charles Napier (1786-1860). Many writers have embodied the main conclusions of the historians we have named, in brief, but useful, histories for the use of the more advanced schools. The more successful of these are the Rev. James Franck Bright and the late John Richard Green. **James Franck Bright** is 1832- master of University College, Oxford, and his "English History for the use of Public Schools" is a work so lucidly and carefully written, that it is entitled to be lifted out of the category of mere text-books, and to take rank as good literature. Still more is this true of Green's "Short History of the English People." **John Richard Green** 1837-1883 was born at Oxford, and educated at Magdalen College School and at Jesus College. For some time he was vicar of St Philip's, Stepney. His "Short History," published in 1874, was speedily adopted in schools, and had an enormous sale among general readers. It was immediately recognised that a brilliant writer had appeared, one who had assimilated all that was worthy in the work of laborious contemporary historians, had himself made much study of original documents, and had welded all together by the power of real genius. A critic here and there devoted himself to discovering the errors, mainly of dates, which, owing to the illness of the author, disfigured the first edition. But the popular instinct which declared this to be a great work, was a sound one. In the main its conclusions are just. There is not a line of cheap sentiment or rhetorical clap-trap in the book. Mr Green soon afterwards enlarged his work, and published it in four handsome volumes, which he dedicated to his friends—" My Masters in the Study of English History,"—Bishop Stubbs and Professor Freeman. Later on appeared " The Making of England," and, after his decease, another volume, " The Conquest of England," written on his deathbed, was published by his widow, Alice Stopford Green, who has written " Town Life in the Fifteenth Century." Sir Archibald Geikie, the geologist, once rendered a tribute to Green for endeavouring to bring geological science to the aid of historical research ; but on the question of the Teutonic element in our nation, it has been urged that Green follows his friends, Stubbs and Freeman, all too readily, and ignores the evidence from anthropology in favour of the very great prevalence of Celtic blood in the English-speaking race.

I regret that my space will not permit me to write at length of the men who have studied so thoroughly sciences which have so much bearing upon history, and who have written delightful books upon them. I must be content merely to mention the names of William Boyd Dawkins, who

Victorian Literature

has written "Cave-hunting" and "Early Man in Britain;" and Sir John Lubbock, banker and member of Parliament, who has written "Prehistoric Times" and "The Origin of Civilization and the Primitive Condition of Man," also various books on natural science, and some very inadequate literary essays. Nor must I forget Edward Burnett Tylor's "Primitive Culture" and "Anthropology," Grant Allen's "Anglo-Saxon Britain," and Edward Clodd's "Childhood of the World," "Childhood of Religion," and "Pioneers of Evolution." From such works as these it is but a very short step to the writings of Max Müller. **Friedrich Max Müller,** son of the 1823- German poet, Wilhelm Müller, was educated at the University of Leipzig, and made a special study of philosophy in Germany for many years before he came to the land of his adoption, in 1846. Appointed an Oxford professor, first of modern languages and later of comparative philology, a science which he may almost be said to have created, he has become an Englishman both in speech and in writing. Max Müller's most popular works are his interesting "Lectures on the Science of Language," and his "Chips from a German Workshop," in which he deals not only with the common origin of the world's leading languages, but in a skilful and almost startling manner reconstructs, by the aid of language alone, the conditions out of which have risen the various religious and social systems of the early nations. The writers who have most prominently followed in Max Müller's footsteps, as elucidators of primitive religious belief, are Professor Sayce and the Rev. Sir George Cox. **Archibald Henry** 1846- **Sayce**, who succeeded Max Müller in the chair of comparative philology at Oxford, has written numerous books and treatises dealing with the Chaldean and other ancient nations, and has also published an annotated edition of Herodotus, noticeable chiefly for its unfavourable verdict on 1827- the "Father of History." **Sir George Cox**, whose "Mythology of the Aryan Nations" has provoked much adverse criticism from its extreme application of the "Solar" theory to the interpretation of myth, epic, and romance, has also written an interesting "History of Greece" in two volumes.

The "History of Greece" which may be considered one of the most satisfactory achievements of the Victorian era, is that by Grote, published in 1794-1871 twelve volumes. **George Grote** was born at Clay Hill, near Beckenham, and was educated at the Charterhouse School. He early went into the banking-house in Threadneedle Street, of which his father was one of the partners, but found time to devote himself to philosophy and history, and to write for the *Westminster Review*, the organ of philosophical Radicalism. It was as a representative of this phase of thought that he was returned as member of Parliament for the city of London in 1833. He sat in the House as one of a small body of philosophical Radicals until 1841, bringing forward annually a resolution in favour of the ballot. He retired from Parliamentary life to devote himself more energetically to his "History of Greece," the first two volumes of which appeared in 1846; the twelfth, and last, which takes us to the death of Alexander the Great, was published in 1856. During the same years, but unknown to Grote, **Connop Thirlwall,** Bishop of St **1797-1875** David's, a former schoolfellow of his, was engaged upon the same task. Each acknowledged the superiority of his rival's work, and Grote said that he should never have written his had Thirlwall's book appeared a few years earlier; but there can be little hesitation in assigning the higher place to Grote. Of Thirlwall it may be said, however, that but for Grote his history would have taken high rank, and would have been a welcome relief from the foolish but once popular work of William Mitford. Thirlwall is also interesting for having translated, in 1825, Schleiermacher's "Essay on St Luke," and thus first introduced German theology into England. Grote's history is a book of high educational value. In it we have all that is best in Herodotus, Thucydides, and the other ancient historians, added to the sound and weighty judgment of a clear-sighted modern critic, exceptionally free from prejudice. It was Grote's great destiny to free the English mind from the erroneous impressions which had so long prevailed as to the real character of the Athenian democracy, and we cannot find elsewhere a truer or juster picture of Athens at the height of her power. A great work on Greek history in later aspects than those of Grote and Thirlwall is "A History of Greece, from its Conquest by the Romans to the Present 1799-1875 Time," by George Finlay. Finlay fought in the Greek War of Independence, and lived for the greater part of his life in Athens.

A number of clergymen besides Dr Thirlwall have shown an able grasp of classical history. Dr Arnold wrote a "History of Rome," based on Niebuhr, which, although interesting, is scarcely 1808-1893 worthy of so great a man. Charles Merivale, Dean of Ely, wrote an admirable summary of Roman history from the foundation of the city in B.C. 753 to the fall of Augustulus in A.D. 476; but his great work is the "History of the Romans under the Empire," which is indispensable for a thorough 1791-1868 appreciation of Gibbon. Henry Hart Milman, Dean of St Paul's, did good service to historical scholarship by his edition of Gibbon's pre-eminent work, and by his own "History of the Jews," "History of Christianity under the Empire," and

Victorian Literature

"Latin Christianity." The nine volumes of this last were called by Dean Stanley "a complete epic and philosophy of mediæval Christianity." Milman is said to have described himself as "the last learned man in the Church," but in the presence of so eminent a scholar as **Mandell Creighton**, Bishop of London, the statement is meaningless. Dr Creighton's great work, "A History of the Papacy From the Great Schism to the Sack of Rome," is of the highest value in the consecutive study of European history; and so also is the work of another clergyman, **George William Kitchin**, Dean of Durham, whose "History of France previous to the Revolution," is very attractively written. 1843-

1827-

A writer who generalises freely from the facts of history, and whose generalisations were once very popular, and, according to Sir Mackenzie Wallace, are still widely read in Russia, was **Henry Thomas Buckle**, who published in 1857 the first volume of the "History of Civilisation in England;" a second volume appeared in 1861, but the author died before he had completed his intended undertaking. Buckle unduly emphasises the influence of national and moral laws upon the progress of civilisation, minimises the influence of individuals, and overlooks the momentous action of heredity. A writer of equal importance with Buckle was **John Addington Symonds**, whose "Renaissance in Italy" is a work of great literary merit, and whose 1821-1862

1840-1893

translation of Cellini's "Autobiography" has superseded Roscoe's.

Passing from historic Italy to Germany we may note that "The Holy Roman Empire" of **James** 1838- **Bryce** created quite a *furore* as a prize essay at Oxford, and, in its enlarged shape, forms the only English sketch of German history of great literary merit. Mr Bryce was, some years ago, announced to write a "History of Germany" of more formidable dimensions, but the glamour of parliamentary life and a seat in the Cabinet have robbed us of a capable historian. Although we are without a satisfactory German history we possess two very solid contributions to such a work. With one of these, Carlyle's "Frederick II.," I shall deal 1834-1895 later; the other is **Sir John Robert Seeley's** "Life and Times of Stein; or, Germany and Prussia in the Napoleonic Age." When this work appeared it was received with high commendation in Germany, but in England with the qualification that it had none of the literary charm of the author's earlier efforts. To such criticism Professor Seeley —he received the professorship of modern history at Cambridge on Kingsley's resignation in 1869— replied in a series of papers entitled "History and Politics," wherein he practically contended that it was the business of historians to be dull, and that brilliant history-writing was, as a matter of fact, little other than fiction. Still, in his lectures on

Victorian Literature

" The Expansion of England" (1883) and "A Short History of Napoleon" (1886) he succeeded in making himself entirely interesting.

The books which gave Sir John Seeley his greatest fame—he received a knighthood in 1893—were not, however, historical, but, in a sense, theological; and with him we find ourselves in the midst of the great religious controversies of the reign. "Ecce Homo; a Survey of the Life and Work of Jesus Christ," was published anonymously in 1865. While censured on many sides on account of its alleged heterodoxy, it drew from opponents unstinted admiration on account of its perfect literary workmanship. One of these opponents was Mr Gladstone, who ventured the prophecy that the author would at a later period write something from a more orthodox standpoint. The prediction was not verified, for in 1882 a further work, "Natural Religion," by the Author of "Ecce Homo," showed still less sympathy with the supernatural side of religion.

Mr Gladstone, who flung himself into this as into so many other controversies, has a fame quite apart from any literary achievement. But whatever posterity may say of his influence on the destinies of the nation which he has helped for so many years to rule, it is certain that his powers as an author would have made the reputation of a man of less versatility.

William Ewart Gladstone, the son of a Lancashire merchant, was born at Liverpool. Into his political career it is not my province to enter. His first literary work, "The State in its Relations with the Church," was made famous through a review by Macaulay. Later in life he indulged in theological controversy, publishing an "Essay on Ritualism" and "The Vatican Decrees." Mr Gladstone's chief work is, however, his "Studies in Homer," in which he argues for the unity of the poem, for the foundation in fact of its main incidents, and for the definite personality of the author. His contributions to periodical literature have been innumerable, and only a few —and those non-controversial and non-classical— have been republished in his five volumes of "Gleanings." Mr Gladstone's chief opponent in theological controversy, Cardinal Newman, has profoundly influenced his religious views. "In my opinion," wrote Mr Gladstone many years after Newman had become a Roman Catholic, "his secession from the Church of England has never yet been estimated among us at anything like the full amount of its calamitous importance. It has been said that the world does not know its greatest men ; neither, I will add, is it aware of the power and weight carried by the words and the acts of those among its greatest men whom it does know. The ecclesiastical historian will perhaps hereafter judge that this secession was a much greater event even than the partial secession of John Wesley, the only case of personal loss suffered by the Church of England since the Reformation which can be at all compared with it in magnitude."

John Henry Newman was born in London, and 1801-1890 educated at a private school at Ealing and at Trinity College, Oxford. Inclined at first to the liberal Christianity which men like Whately and Milman were furthering among churchmen, he was, he says, "rudely awakened by two great blows—illness and bereavement"; and he devoted himself to a life-long opposition to what he has called "the great apostasy—liberalism in religion." "My battle," he writes, "was with liberalism; by liberalism I mean the anti-dogmatic principle and its developments." From 1828 to 1843 he held the incumbency of St Mary's Church, Oxford, and the influence which he then exerted was of the deepest moment for the future of religious life in England. "Who," says Matthew Arnold, himself, like his father before him, one of the leaders of the movement which Newman has hated so intensely, "who could resist the charm of that spiritual apparition, gliding in the dim afternoon light through the aisles of St Mary's, rising into the pulpit, and then, in the most entrancing of voices, breaking the silence with words and thoughts which were a religious music—subtle, sweet, mournful? I seem to hear him still, saying: 'After the fever of life, after wearinesses and sicknesses, fightings and despondings, languor and fretfulness, struggling and succeeding; after all the changes and chances of this troubled, unhealthy state,—at length comes death, at length the white .throne of God, at length the beatific vision.'" During these years at St Mary's what is called the Tractarian movement sprang to life—a movement, as we have said, against Broad-Churchism. It was at the beginning of the movement, on his way home from Sicily in 1833, whilst pondering over the difficulties of the task he had undertaken, that Newman wrote the hymn "Lead, kindly Light," which is now as popular in the most advanced and liberalized churches as it can be in those nearest to its author's religious standpoint. The "Tracts for the Times," whence Tractarians derived their name, were written by Newman, Hurrell Froude, Pusey, and others. Bishop Bloomfield said that the whole movement was nothing but Newmania. The writers argued now in short papers, now in elaborate treatises, for the Divine mission of the Anglican Church. Not till "Tract XC." was reached did the alarm of the Protestant party manifest itself in any practical form. In that Tract Newman declared that subscription to the Thirty-nine Articles was not inconsistent with the acceptance of Roman Catholic teaching on purgatory, on the invocation of saints, and on the mass. The Hebdomadal Council of the University condemned the Tract. Two years later Newman resigned his position at St Mary's, and in 1845 formally joined the Church of Rome. According to Disraeli, Anglicanism "reeled under the shock," and Dean Stanley remarked to a friend that the fortunes of the English Church might have been very different "had Newman been able to read German." [1]

In 1848 he was appointed head of the Birmingham Oratory, and there he resided—with one short break as rector of the Roman Catholic University at Dublin—for nearly forty years. In 1879 he was created a cardinal, and his visit to Rome and installation as a Prince of the Sacred College excited much attention in England. Although by temperament and inclination one of the least combative and most retiring of men, Cardinal Newman found himself again and again in the thick of the argumentative fray. At one time he was involved in a libel action by an ex-priest and ultra-Protestant lecturer named Father Achilli, and this cost Newman and his friends twelve thousand pounds; at another time he was arguing with the foremost English statesman, Mr Gladstone, as to the probable loyalty of English Roman Catholics if the Papacy and the English Government were brought into collision. In one great controversy of his life

[1] " Memoirs of Mark Pattison."

he was generally admitted to have achieved a success, and this success is associated with an enduring literary work, the autobiography which he calls his " Apologia pro Vitâ Suâ." Reviewing Froude's " History of England " in *Macmillan's Magazine* (January 1864), Charles Kingsley charged Newman with being careless about truth, and with teaching that cunning and not truth-seeking was the acceptable method of the Roman Catholic clergy. Brought to bay by Newman, Kingsley contradicted himself in an amazing fashion, and even the most enthusiastic Protestants were compelled to admit that the clever novelist was no match for the trained dialectician. Mrs Kingsley, in her charming life of her husband, practically admits that he was worsted in the conflict, and J. A. Froude, his brother-in-law, wrote : " Kingsley entirely misunderstood Newman's character. Newman's whole life had been a struggle for truth. He had neglected his own interests ; he had never thought of them at all. He had brought to bear a most powerful and subtle intellect to support the convictions of a conscience which was superstitiously sensitive. His single object had been to discover what were the real relations between man and his Maker, and to shape his own conduct by the conclusions at which he arrived. To represent such a person as careless of truth was neither generous nor even reasonable."

Victorian Literature

The final outcome of the controversy was the publication of the "Apologia," a work which, alike in beauty of style and devotion of spirit, must be assigned a very high place in religious literature. My space is too limited to pass in review, or even to name, the thirty-six volumes which contain the writings of this eloquent preacher and teacher. His "Dream of Gerontius" and "Verses on Various Occasions" show his high qualities as a poet; his "Apologia," "Callista," and "Essay in aid of the Grammar of Assent," display his genius as a prose stylist. In "Callista : a Sketch of the Third Century," he pictures a beautiful Greek girl, who becomes a convert to Christianity after a severe struggle between human affection and religious faith. The "Grammar of Assent" is an apology for Christianity, far above the narrow controversies in which the author took so distinguished a part.

The question whether Cardinal Newman or Carlyle has been the most influential personality in Victorian literature will be largely decided by the temperament of the critic. Mr Swinburne, looking at them both from a standpoint of antagonism to the priestly proclivities of the one and to the tyrannical proclivities of the other, apostrophised them jointly in the well-known lines :—

Sixty Years of

" With all our hearts we praise you whom ye hate,
　　High souls that hate us ; for our hopes are higher,
　　And higher than yours the goal of our desire,
　Though high your ends be as your hearts are great."

Newman, indeed, left England more dominated
by ritual than in any other period of its history,
the Roman Church more powerful than ever before, the new High Church party in the Establish-
ment a great institution, with the rival Prime
Ministers, Mr Gladstone and Lord Salisbury,
among its supporters, and a taste for ritual conspicuous in the chapels of the Nonconformists.
And yet with all this Carlyle was the more
dominant personality.

1795-1881 **Thomas Carlyle** was born at Ecclefechan, in
Dumfriesshire, on the 4th of December 1795.
His father was a stonemason, at whose death
Carlyle thus tenderly wrote in his Diary :— " I
owe him much more than existence. I owe him
a noble inspiring example. It was he *exclusively*
that determined on educating me; that from his
small hard-earned funds sent me to school and
college, and made me whatever I am and may
become. Let me not mourn for my father, let me
do worthily of him. So shall he still live, even
here in me, and his worth plant itself honourably
forth into new generations." From Annan Grammar School the young Carlyle went to Edinburgh
University, where he became a voracious reader,

although never a great classical scholar. He then took the post of mathematical tutor at Annan school, and afterwards at Kirkcaldy, where he was friendly with Edward Irving, afterwards the famous preacher. Disgusted with this life he flung up his appointment, and determined to study for the law. For some time he eked out a scanty subsistence in Edinburgh by writing biographies for Brewster's *Encyclopædia*. It was at this period that he obtained some measure of mental and moral stimulus from his German studies. Goethe opened a new world to him. He began to study German in 1819, induced thereto by Madame de Staël's interesting account of the German poets and philosophers. Goethe was seventy-five years old when in 1824 he received from Carlyle an English translation of "Wilhelm Meister," with a letter, saying, "Four years ago, when I read your 'Faust' among the mountains of my native Scotland, I could not but fancy I might one day see you, and pour out before you, as before a father, the woes and wanderings of a heart whose mysteries you seemed so thoroughly to comprehend, and could so beautifully represent." Two years later Carlyle sent Goethe his "Life of Schiller," and once again he expressed his intense devotion to one "whose voice came to me from afar, with counsel and help, in my utmost need." "For if," he continues, "I have been delivered from darkness into any measure of light, if I know aught of myself and my destination, it is to the study of your writings more than to any other circumstance that I owe this ; it is you more than any other man that I should always thank and reverence with the feeling of a disciple to his Master, nay, of a son to his spiritual Father." In the meantime Carlyle had married Jane Welsh, the daughter of a doctor in Haddington, and had settled at the lonely farm-house of Craigenputtock, in Dumfriesshire. There he was visited by Emerson, and there he remained for six years, before removing to London. Not only had Carlyle then translated "Wilhelm Meister" and written the "Life of Schiller," but he had made numerous translations from Musæus, Tieck, and Richter, and had published essays on these and other German authors. Jean Paul Richter had a peculiar attraction for him, and there can be no doubt that Carlyle owed his extraordinary style, in some degree, to his study of the German humorist.

The forty-seven years of Carlyle's London life (1834-1881) were years of incessant literary activity. The thirty volumes which came from his pen during that time not only secured for him a permanent place amongst the historians, biographers, and essayists of our literature, but they kindled for him a glow of intense personal enthusiasm amongst the best of his contemporaries, such as, perhaps, no other English author has enjoyed. At his death on the 5th of February, 1881, the world knew Carlyle, apart from his books, as a man of simple tastes, content, in spite of the wealth which literary success had brought, to reside amidst unostentatious surroundings, ever ready to help the distressed and needy, refusing a title and the like official recognitions, and carrying out to the letter the reverence, earnestness, and unobtrusive manliness which he had inculcated in his writings; devotedly attached to his wife, whom he described on her tombstone as having " unweariedly forwarded him as none else could, in all of good that he did or attempted ;" and, in short, worthy of the address presented to him on his eightieth birthday, by nearly all the men of literary and scientific eminence in England, including, amongst others, Lord Tennyson and George Eliot, Robert Browning and Professor Huxley. " A whole generation has elapsed," they said, " since you described for us the hero as a man of letters. We congratulate you and ourselves on the spacious fulness of years which has enabled you to sustain this rare dignity amongst mankind in all its possible splendour and completeness." The publication of Mr Froude's nine volumes of memorials caused a considerable revulsion of feeling. The Carlyle of these " Letters" and " Reminiscences " appeared to be over-censorious in his estimate of his contemporaries, not too considerate in his relations with his wife, and, however admirable he might find contentment in Richter or Heyne, not content without much murmuring to accept a life of restricted means.

To give too much emphasis to this view of Carlyle's character is to ignore certain peculiarities of Mr Froude's biographical and historical style, to which reference has already been made. It will suffice to point out here that there are other sources of information about Carlyle than the books of his accredited biographer. Sir Henry Taylor, Mrs Oliphant, Mr Charles Eliot Norton, Mrs Gilchrist, and other friends of Carlyle's later life have published much additional matter, and have shown, as it were, the other side of the shield. To Sir Henry Taylor, who knew him well, he seemed "the most faithful and true-hearted of men," and from many sources we learn that Mr Froude's picture is not that of the true Carlyle; that he was not a selfish husband, that his married life was not unhappy, that he was not altogether dumb to the heroes living, whilst eloquent over heroes dead, and that, in spite of many faults, he was a noble high-minded man, a "kingly soul," as Longfellow called him. Writing in his Diary during his second visit to England in 1847, Emerson says :—"Carlyle and his wife live on beautiful terms. Their ways are very engaging, and in her bookcase all his books are inscribed to her as they came from year to year, each with some significant lines."

The letters which Carlyle wrote to his wife at the time she lost her mother are most touchingly affectionate. This is what she wrote to a friend at that time :—" In great matters he is always kind and considerate, but these little attentions which we women attach so much importance to, he was never in the habit of rendering to anyone. And, now, the desire to replace the irreplaceable makes him as good in little things as he used to be in great." And to Carlyle himself she writes :— " God keep you, my dear husband, and bring you safe back to me. The house looks very desolate without you, and my mind feels empty too. I expect, with impatience, the letter that is to fix your return."

On another occasion, writing to her husband's mother, she says :—" You have others behind and I have only him—only him in the whole wide world to love me and take care of me—poor little wretch that I am. Not but that numbers of people love me, after their fashion, far more than I deserve, but then his fashion is so different from theirs, and seems alone to suit the crotchety creature that I am." And then her pride in her husband is well exemplified by an experience related in a letter to him, which shows also how wide and deep is that mysterious impersonal influence of great authors on men who are totally unknown to them:—" A man of the people mounted the platform and spoke ; a youngish, intelligent-looking man, who alone, of all the speakers, seemed to understand the question, and to have feelings as well as notions about it. He spoke with a heart-eloquence that left me warm. I never was more affected by public speaking. . . . A sudden thought struck me : this man would like to know you. I would give him my address in London. I borrowed a piece of paper and handed him my address. When he looked at it he started as if I had sent a bullet into him, caught my hand, and said, 'Oh, it is your husband ! Mr Carlyle has been my teacher and master ! I have owed everything to him for years and years !' I felt it a credit to you really to have had a hand in turning out this man, was prouder of that heart-tribute to your genius than any amount of reviewers' praises or aristocratic invitations to dinner."

It is because the spirit which breathes in the words of this young workman has been the guiding moral force of numbers of men and women in all stations of life, during the last sixty years, that I have devoted so much space to Carlyle. It is of the greatest importance to literature that the man whose eloquent preaching of justice, sincerity, and reverence has turned the hearts of thousands of his fellowmen towards nobility and simplicity of life, should not himself have been out of harmony with all that he taught. "The world," says Thackeray's gifted daughter, "has pointed its moral finger of late at the old man in his great old age, accusing himself in the face of all, and confessing the overpowering irritations which the suffering of a lifetime had laid upon him and upon her he loved. That old caustic man of deepest feeling, with an ill-temper and a tender heart, and a racking imagination, speaking from the grave, and bearing unto it that cross of passionate remorse which few among us dare to face, seems to some of us now a figure nobler and truer, a teacher greater far than in the days when all his pain and love and remorse were still hidden from us all."[1]

Of the " Reminiscences " which excited so much criticism on account of their references to persons still living, Carlyle wrote on the last page:—" I still mainly mean to *burn* this book before my own departure, but feel that I shall always have a kind of grudge to do it, and an indolent excuse. ' Not *yet;* wait, any day that can be done!' and that it *is* possible the thing *may* be left behind me, legible to interested survivors—*friends* only, I will hope, and with *worthy* curiosity, not *un*worthy! In which event, I solemnly forbid them, each and all, to *publish* this bit of writing *as it stands here,* and

[1] Mrs Thackeray-Ritchie, *Harper's Magazine* (1883).

warn them that *without fit editing* no *part* of it should be printed (nor so far as I can order *shall* ever be), and that the 'fit editing' of perhaps nine-tenths of it will, after I am gone, have become *impossible.*" [1]

The only editing which Mr Froude deemed "fit" was the omission of this paragraph from his edition of the work. And yet to read, with the "worthy curiosity" of which he speaks, of his love for father and wife, and of his kindly solicitude for brothers and sisters, whom he constantly assisted, is to make him nearer and dearer to those who care to remember that he was after all but human. Carlyle spoke with too little kindness, it must be owned, of Wordsworth, and Coleridge, and Lamb, because he saw only the palpable weaknesses of their characters, and was blinded by forbidding externals to the sterling worth of these great men; but he loved Emerson, and Tennyson, and Ruskin, and he profoundly revered Goethe, who, after all, was the only one of his contemporaries who could take rank anywhere near him. [2] Carlyle recognised that Goethe was incomparably his

[1] "Reminiscences," by Thomas Carlyle. 2nd Edition. Edited by C. E. Norton (1887).

[2] When George Eliot read Carlyle's eulogy on Emerson in introducing his essays to the British public, she wrote :— "I have shed many tears over it : this is a world worth abiding in while one man can thus venerate and love another."— Cross's "Life of George Eliot."

superior in every way; that he was, as Matthew
Arnold calls him, "the greatest poet of the present
age, and the greatest critic of all ages," the one
man of transcendent genius whom Europe has
produced since Dante and Shakspere. To have
first led England to appreciate Goethe is not the
least of Carlyle's many services to his country. To
have acted as an inspiring and helpful prophet is
perhaps his greatest. "Sartor Resartus" first appeared in *Fraser's Magazine* for 1833, where it
met with but scanty recognition, and, indeed, half-
ruined the editor, whose subscribers anxiously
asked when the "tailor sketches" were coming to
an end. It is surely something more than a passing fashion in literature which leads us now to take
up these well-worn pages with so much of tenderness and sympathy. "There is in man," he says,
"a Higher than Love of Happiness; he can do
without Happiness, and instead thereof find
Blessedness! Was it not to preach forth this
same Higher that sages and martyrs, the Poet and
the Priest, in all times, have spoken and suffered;
bearing testimony, through life and through death,
of the Godlike that is in Man, and how, in the
Godlike only, has he Strength and Freedom?"
How can it be said that Carlyle did not love
humanity when we read the lines in which he
expresses reverence for the "toilworn Craftsman
that, with earth-made Implement, laboriously con-

quers the Earth and makes her man's?" "Venerable to me," he continues, "is the hard Hand; crooked, coarse; wherein notwithstanding lies a cunning virtue, indefeasibly royal, as of the Sceptre of this Planet. Venerable, too, is the rugged face, all weather-tanned, besoiled, with its rude intelligence; for it is the face of a Man living manlike. O, but the more venerable for thy rudeness, and even because we must pity as well as love thee! Hardly entreated Brother! For us was thy back so bent, for us were thy straight limbs and fingers so deformed; thou wert our Conscript on whom the lot fell, and fighting our battles wert so marred."

It is impossible to exaggerate the effect upon the younger minds of his age of Carlyle's stirring words, inciting to worthy and ever worthier effort: —"Do the duty which lies nearest to thee, which thou knowest to be a duty. In all situations out of the pit of Tophet, wherein a living man has stood, there is actually a prize of quite infinite value placed within his reach, namely a duty for him to do; this highest of Gospels forms the basis and worth of all other gospels whatever." "Brother," he says elsewhere, "thou hast possibility in thee for much, the possibility of writing on the eternal skies the record of a heroic life. Is not every man, God be thanked, a potential hero? The measure of a nation's greatness, of its worth under the sky to God and to man, is not the quantity of bullion it has realised, but the quantity of heroisms it has achieved, of noble pieties and valiant wisdoms that were in it, that still are in it."

Little less valuable than "Sartor Resartus" is "Past and Present," which was published in 1843. The reverence and delicacy with which it touches the monasticism of a bygone age are as remarkable as the prophetic vision with which it deals with the social problems of our latter-day life. State-aided emigration, co-operation and national education, are some of the many changes advocated here and elsewhere. Not till the "Latter-day Pamphlets" (1850) did Carlyle become an eloquent advocate of "force" as a guide in politics, thereby alienating John Stuart Mill and many of his old friends. His language then seemed to degenerate into mere shrieking and scolding. The world must be governed, he declared, by men of heroic mould, who know what is good for the inferior natures around them. Let such inferior natures, if need be, be scourged into silence. Parliaments he spoke of contemptuously as "talking shops," and his sympathies went out heartily to Governor Eyre at the time of the Jamaica riots, and to the Southern States at the time of the American Civil War. An admiration for "heaven-sent heroes" had always been strong in Carlyle, although it certainly had not its after meaning when he wrote in early life, "Not brute force, but only persuasion and faith are the kings of this world." In "Heroes and Hero-worship," a course of lectures delivered in 1840, he had waxed eloquent over Mahomet, Luther, and Napoleon, and three years earlier, in 1837, he had published in his "French Revolution" a brilliant eulogy of Mirabeau. His vindication of Cromwell was brought about perhaps mainly by his appreciation of the Protector's high-handed resoluteness, and his "Life of Frederick II. of Prussia" was the apology for a man who was the very embodiment of despotic ideals.

But quite apart from Carlyle's worth as a moral teacher or as a controversialist, his place in literature is very high. His short biography of Schiller was an epoch-making book, because of the influence it has exercised upon the study of German literature : but it bears little evidence of the genius of its author, and, in consequence of the abundance of Schiller correspondence subsequently brought to light, it has been superseded by the biographies of Palleskie and Duntzer. Carlyle's "Life of John Sterling" is, however, a work of great power, a kind of prose "Lycidas," which, like that great elegy, has rescued from oblivion a man in whom the world would soon have ceased to be interested. Carlyle, again, was an essayist of striking individu-

Victorian Literature

ality. Few literary sketches are more picturesque
than his "Count Cagliostro" and "The Diamond
Necklace," and the essays on Johnson and Burns
are models of generous human insight. With
literary insight, however, Carlyle was not too well
endowed, at least, when purely imaginative literature was concerned, and he once expressed the
opinion that Shakspere had better have written in
prose. "It is part of my creed," he wrote to
Emerson, "that the only poetry is history could
we tell it right." His method of telling it gives
him a place by himself among historians, a place
so singular that it is impossible to classify him.
"Carlyle's 'French Revolution,'" said John Stuart
Mill, "is one of those productions of genius which
is above all rule, and is a law to itself." The
deathbed of Louis XV., the taking of the Bastille,
and the execution of Danton, are never-to-be-for-
gotten descriptions, and the poetical passage which
follows the relation of the bloody horrors of 1789
cannot be too often quoted:—"O evening sun of
July, how, at this hour, thy beams fall slant on
reapers amid peaceful woody fields; on old women
spinning in cottages; on ships far out in the silent
main; on Balls at the Orangerie of Versailles,
where high-rouged Dames of the Palace are even
now dancing with double-jacketed Hussar-Officers;
—and also on this roaring Hell-porch of a Hôtel-
de-Ville!"

The scientific history of the French Revolution has yet to be written; and even to appreciate Carlyle's prose epic adequately we should know something of Mignet, Thiers, Morse Stephens, and von Sybel, but neither the accumulation of fresh facts, nor a philosophical deduction from such facts, can impair the value of Carlyle's work. That, in spite of all his fire and passion, Carlyle could delineate character with most judicial fairness, may be demonstrated by turning to Mr John Morley's essays on Robespierre and the other revolutionists, and observing how his calm and unprejudiced intellect has pronounced judgments in every way endorsing Carlyle's.

Carlyle's "Cromwell" has less attraction for us to-day than the "French Revolution"; but the service to historical study was even greater. Opinions will always differ as to the wisdom of the Protector's policy and the righteousness of his deeds, but since the publication of these letters and speeches, "edited with the care of an antiquarian and the genius of a poet," [1] Cromwell's sincerity and genuine piety have been unimpugned. There are others beside Mr Froude who esteem the "History of Frederick II." Carlyle's greatest work. The humour of the book is wonderful, for Carlyle is the greatest humorist since Sterne, and nowhere is this humour more conspicuous than in

[1] Green's "Short History of the English People."

Victorian Literature

"Frederick." The splendid portraits of all the
most important figures in the eighteenth century
fix themselves indelibly in the memory, and it is
even said that German soldiers study the art of
war from the descriptions of Frederick's campaigns.
Nevertheless, the book has much in it that is un-
satisfying to Englishmen. Frederick and his father
could not easily excite the hero-worshipping in
clinations of a free people, and even Carlyle became
disillusioned as he proceeded with his task, and
finally admitted that Frederick was not worth the
trouble he had given to him. He commenced it
as a "History of Frederick the Great,' and concluded it as a "History of Frederick, *called* the
Great."

Carlyle is surely the greatest figure in our
modern literature. He wrote no poetry worth
consideration, it is true. His verse would long
since have been forgotten had it not been for
his effectiveness as a prose writer. But although
we are accustomed to the claim for poetry that
it ranks higher than prose, it must be conceded
that in Victorian literature this is not the case,
and that Carlyle's enormous personality, his
capacity for influencing others for good and ill,
have made him the greatest moral and intellectual
force of his age. To him we owe the indiffer-
ence to mere political shibboleths, the lull in

party warfare, which is the note of our age. He gave no definite answer to any question, but he gave us the impetus which led others to seek for solutions. His literary influence on Froude and Mill, Mr Ruskin and Mr Lecky, and numbers of others was tremendous. The place which was occupied by Swift in the eighteenth century is held by Carlyle in the nineteenth, and though every line that he has written should cease to be read, he will still be remembered as the greatest of literary figures in an age of great men of letters.

CHAPTER IV

The Critics

THE plan of describing all the writers of a period who are not poets, novelists and historians as critics is open to many objections, although I intend to adopt it. If Matthew Arnold's plea for poetry as a criticism of life holds good, it is precisely the poets, novelists and historians who are the true critics. An alternative plan would have been to give a chapter to prose writers and another to the poets; and still another arrangement would have been to divide the subject, as De Quincey suggested, into the literature of power and the literature of imagination, the former including the philosophers and historians, the latter the poets, the novelists, and the more picturesque of the prose writers — Carlyle and Ruskin, for example.

One unhesitatingly assigns to Mr Ruskin the distinction of the critic whose work is most eloquent and impressive. **John Ruskin** was born 1819- in Hunter Street, Brunswick Square, London.

He has told us in his autobiography, "Præterita," of his early life under a tender mother's care, of his boyish affection for Byron and Scott, and of the youthful impulse to art study excited by the present of Rogers's "Italy," with Turner's illustrations. In 1837 he was entered as a gentleman commoner at Christ Church, Oxford, gaining, two years later, the Newdigate prize for English poetry, his subject being "Salsette and Elephanta." In 1843 he produced the first volume of "Modern Painters: their Superiority in the Art of Landscape Painting to all the Ancient Masters. By a Graduate of Oxford." The work originated, he says, "in indignation at the shallow and false criticism of the periodicals of the day on the work of the great living artist to whom it principally refers." The artist in question was Joseph Mallord William Turner, upon whom Ruskin has pronounced somewhat contradictory judgments at different periods in his career. "Modern Painters" soon extended beyond the mere essay at first intended, and in its final form of five handsome volumes, it was not only a philosophical treatise on landscape painting, but an exhaustive dissertation on many phases of life from one whom Mazzini declared to possess "the most analytic brain in Europe."

Another important work, "The Seven Lamps of Architecture" (1849), is a brilliant attempt at re-

form in domestic and church architecture. The
"lamps" represent the characteristics which good
architecture should possess. The first is the Lamp
of Sacrifice : "What of beauty and what of riches
we may possess, let a portion be dedicated to God.
It was in this spirit that our cathedrals were built."
The second, the Lamp of Truth, is a plea for
honesty in architecture, no imitation wood or
marble, but solid wood and solid stone. "Exactly
as a woman of feeling," he says, "would not wear
false jewels, so would a builder of honour disdain
false ornaments. The using of them is just as
downright and inexcusable a lie." The third is
the Lamp of Power : "Until that street architecture of ours is bettered, until we give it some
size and boldness, until we give our windows recess
and our walls thickness, I know not how we can
blame our architects for their feebleness in more
important work." The fourth is the Lamp of
Beauty, and in this chapter he maintains that "all
the most lovely forms and thoughts" are directly
taken from natural objects. The fifth is the Lamp
of Life. "To those who love architecture," he
says, "the life and accent of the hand are everything." The sixth is the Lamp of Memory : "All
public edifices should be records of national life,
all ordinary dwelling-houses endeared to their
owners by sacred and sweet associations. There
is infinite sanctity in a good man's house !" The

seventh is the Lamp of Obedience, and here he pleads eloquently for the enforcement of an established type of architecture—the Gothic, in his judgment, lending itself most readily to all services, vulgar or noble. The "Stones of Venice" (1851-1853), in three volumes, gives in further detail Ruskin's views of the laws of architecture. The pre-Raphaelite movement of Millais, Rossetti, and Holman Hunt early enlisted his sympathy, and in "Pre-Raphaelitism" (1851) he declared that they had worthily followed the advice given in "Modern Painters," to "go to nature in all singleness of heart, and walk with her laboriously and trustingly, having no other thought but how best to penetrate her meaning; rejecting nothing, selecting nothing, and scorning nothing." From that time until his Slade lectures at Oxford in 1883-1884 Ruskin wrote several books on painting and architecture, all of them in a style which attracts even those who are least in sympathy with his opinions.

But as Goethe declared of himself that posterity would honour him, not for his poetry, but for his discoveries in science, so Ruskin, perhaps more justly, insists that it is as an economist that he is most deserving of remembrance. The four essays on the first principles of political economy, entitled "Unto this Last" (1862), he declares to be "the truest, rightest-worded, and most serviceable things " he has ever written. These essays were originally published by Thackeray in the *Cornhill Magazine*, but the remonstrances of its readers brought the series to a speedy end. The principles of state socialism there initiated have since entered the field in direct contest with the established order of things. Mr Ruskin would have every child in the country taught a trade at the cost of government ; he would have manufactories and workshops entirely under government regulation for the production and sale of every necessary of life, and for the exercise of every useful art ; he would permit competition with government manufactories and shops, but all who desired work could be sure of it at the state establishments : finally, he would provide comfortable homes for the old and destitute, as "it ought to be quite as natural and straightforward a matter for a labourer to take his pension from his parish, because he has deserved well of his parish, as for a man in higher rank to take his pension from his country because he has deserved well of his country." Ruskin has amplified his economic doctrines in "Munera Pulveris," "Time and Tide by Wear and Tyne," and "Fors Clavigera." "Time and Tide" is a collection of letters on the laws of work to the late Thomas Dixon, a working corkcutter of Sunderland. They were originally published in the *Manchester Examiner*. "Fors Clavigera" is a series of ninety-

six letters to working-men, which were issued
in monthly parts, and rendered additionally
interesting by the quantity of autobiographical
anecdotes so freely interspersed in their pages.
The title is derived, as Ruskin has explained, from
the Latin *fors*, the best part of three good English
words—force, fortitude, and fortune ; the root of
the adjective *clavigera* being either *clava*, a club,
clavis, a key, or *clavus*, a nail, and *gero*, to carry.
Fors the Club-bearer therefore represents the
strength of Hercules or of Deed ; the Key-bearer,
the strength of Ulysses or of Patience ; and the
Nail-bearer, the strength of Lycurgus or of Law.

To carry out his principles practically, Ruskin
established for a short time a tea shop in the
Marylebone Road, where nothing but the best tea
was sold at a fair price, and he founded the St
George's Guild with a view of showing "the rational
organisation of country life independent of that of
cities ;" or in other words, the restoration of the
peasantry to the soil of England. One of the
conditions of membership was that every member
should give one-tenth of his property to the guild
for carrying out its work. Ruskin led the way, his
property being then estimated at £70,000. He
has told us in "Fors" that out of the £157,000 left
him by his parents he has spent £153,000. Much
of this must have gone to the Ruskin Museum at
Sheffield.

Victorian Literature

It is, however, in following Carlyle as a bracing, invigorating influence that Ruskin has most claim on the gratitude of the present generation. If Carlyle taught us to be content with this "miserable actual," with such environment as may have fallen to our lot, his disciple has given the impulse which has led to the beautifying of that environment. The more refined taste in dress, furniture, and in dwelling-houses which has characterized the later Victorian era, and, side by side therewith, a greater simplicity of life on the part of the more cultured rich, are in an especial degree due to the influence of Ruskin. "What is chiefly needed in England at the present day," he says, "is to show the quantity of pleasure that may be obtained by a consistent, well-administered competence, modest, confessed, and laborious. We need examples of people who, leaving Heaven to decide whether they are to rise in the world, decide for themselves that they will be happy in it, and have resolved to seek—not greater wealth, but simpler pleasures ; not higher fortune, but deeper felicity ; making the first of possessions, self-possession ; and honouring themselves in the harmless pride and calm pursuits of peace." In the "Crown of Wild Olive," "Time and Tide," and "Sesame and Lilies," he emphasizes this teaching with his customary eloquence. Of these books, by far the most important is "Sesame and Lilies," which was written, he says, "while my energies were still unbroken and my temper unfretted, and if read in connection with 'Unto this Last,' contains the chief truths I have endeavoured through all my life to display, and which, under the warnings I have received to prepare for its close, I am chiefly thankful to have learnt and taught." It treats of "the majesty of the influence of good books and of good women, if we know how to read them and how to honour." How to read books he shows by analyzing the well-known passage from Milton's "Lycidas" on "The Pilot of the Galilean Lake," and explaining the deep meaning of its every word. How to honour women, how women may become worthy of honour, he shows by taking us to Shakspere and to Scott, whose Portias and Rosalinds, Catherine Seytons and Diana Vernons are ever ready at critical moments to be a help and a guidance to men; and finally he appeals to the great Florentine, and shows us Beatrice leading Dante through the starry spheres of heaven up to the very throne of light and of truth. But the book is full of healthy and helpful passages, and is, like so much that its author has written, a moral inspiration for all who read it. "I am a great man," Ruskin once said, with a consciousness of genius which reminds us that Horace and Milton, Shakspere and Goethe were equally outspoken. Posterity, we may well believe, will endorse the self-criticism, and will not willingly let his works or his memory die.

Of late years Mr Ruskin has lived, not in the most robust health, in a house at Coniston, in the English Lake District.

The next most prominent critic of the period is one upon whom Ruskin has always poured his bitterest scorn, and who yet will be ever remembered with warmest reverence by those who are old enough to have been his contemporaries. I mean John Stuart Mill.

Jeremy Bentham, who gave such an impulse to all political reform, and made a complete revolution in English jurisprudence, died in 1832. His friend James Mill, who wrote the "History of India" and an "Analysis of the Human Mind," died four years later. "It was," says Professor Bain, "James Mill's greatest contribution to human progress to have given us his son." It may be so, and yet he seems to have done his utmost to spoil the gift, not, as children are usually spoiled, by over-indulgence, but by the most excessive severity.

John Stuart Mill was born in Rodney Street, 1806-1873 Pentonville. His education, which was conducted by his father, would have been the mental ruin of a mind of smaller powers. "I never was a boy," he said, "never played at cricket; it is better to let Nature have her own way." He began Greek at three, and Latin at eight

years of age. The list of classical authors with
whose works he was familiar at thirteen is truly
appalling. This in itself would have been a
small matter had not his cold, stern father dis-
couraged all imaginative reading. Poetry in particular he was taught to look upon as mere vanity,
and there are few passages in Mill's "Autobiography" more interesting than the story how in
early manhood Wordsworth's poetry came to him
like veritable "balm in Gilead," for spiritual
refreshment and healing. In 1823 he obtained a
clerkship in the India House, from which he with-
drew, with ample compensation, when the Indian
Government was transferred to the Crown in 1858.
Meanwhile he had been an industrious contributor
to the *Westminster Review* and other periodicals,
and regularly attended the debates of the Speculative Society which met at Grote's house. Scarcely
any scene in literature is better known than the
destruction of the manuscript of Carlyle's "French
Revolution" which he had lent to Mill. Mill lent
it to Mrs Taylor, the lady who afterwards became
his wife, and it was inadvertently destroyed. The
speechless agony of Mill when he went to inform
his friend, the self-command with which Carlyle
and his wife concealed their own misery in endeavouring to moderate his self-reproaches—
these and many other details have been made
familiar to us by many pens. Mill gave Carlyle

what monetary compensation he could, and acted, as he always acted in life, with all possible nobleness. Mrs Taylor, who was the real culprit on this occasion, was the wife of a wholesale druggist in Mark Lane. When Mill made her acquaintance, his father remonstrated, but he replied that he had no other feelings towards her than he would have towards an equally able man. The equivocal friendship, which was the talk of all Mill's circle of acquaintances, lasted for twenty years, when Mr Taylor died, and Mill married his widow. It is impossible to regard the enthusiasm of Mill for this lady without feeling how much there was in it of the humorous, how much also of the pathetic. That Mill had a most exaggerated opinion of her intellectual attainments there can be no doubt. He declared her to be the author of all that was best in his writings. Much of his "Political Economy," he said, was her work, and also the "Liberty" and the "Subjection of Women." His language with regard to her was always extravagant, and Grote said that "only John Mill's reputation could survive such displays." Mill's brother George declared that she was "nothing like what John thought her," and there is much evidence to show that she was but a weak reflection of her husband. Still, it is impossible not to sympathize with such an illusion. Mrs Mill died in 1858, and was buried at Avignon, in France, where Mill himself spent many of the later years of his life, and where he died in 1873. It was at Avignon that the Crown Princess of Prussia and the Princess Alice of Hesse proposed to visit him, when he, with due courtesy, declined to see them.

Mill's works, which are very extensive, deal with philosophical, psychological, economical, and political problems. His "Logic" was published in 1843, his "Essays on Unsettled Questions in Political Economy" in 1844, his "Principles of Political Economy" in 1848, and his "Liberty" in 1858. In 1865 he published his "Examination of Sir William Hamilton's Philosophy." Four volumes of "Dissertations and Discussions" appeared between 1859 and 1867, and "Considerations on Representative Government" in 1861. In 1865 he entered Parliament as Member for Westminster, losing his seat, however, in 1868. It would be hard to speak too highly of Mill. As a man he was all kindliness and considerate thoughtfulness for others, and his ideal of life was a very high one. Carlyle's Letters, Caroline Fox's Memoirs, and many other sources of information, make this clear. On the literary side he will be variously estimated, as we survey him from one or other aspect of his many-sided career. As a stimulator of public opinion the work he did was enormous. This is not the place to discuss the value of this or that movement associated with his name; but there can be no doubt that many questions, like the reform of the land laws, were initiated by him. In the seventies his philosophy dominated Oxford. It is of no account to-day.

On the philosophical side Mill's position is weakened by his ignorance of the more simple sciences, which we now know to be of the greatest moment in the study of intellectual problems. Mill knew little of physics, and of biology still less. His education in this respect belonged to the old-fashioned type. His work in logic is all but unshaken, although his book has been superseded for school and college use. His psychology, however, his ethics, much of his economics, and above all, his metaphysics, must be corrected by later ideas. Doubtless Mill's readjustments in mental science are most valuable, especially his rehandling of the old doctrines; but fundamentally these are Hume's. Mill's chief philosophical work was destructive. He utterly routed the remnants of a still earlier philosophy, furbished up with all the knowledge and all the acuteness of Sir William Hamilton. But the great generalizations which have changed the whole drift of our philosophy are the Conservation of Energy, and Evolution, including as the latter does the laws and conditions of life, and in particular the doctrine of Heredity. For adequate philosophical guidance on these subjects we must turn to Herbert Spencer.

But first let me point to the number of political economists who have followed Mill in the discussion of the relation of society to the "wealth" it produces. Mill's "Political Economy" was more of a systematic summary of the prevailing doctrines than an original work. It long formed, however, the basis of ordinary English knowledge on the subject, and by its adhesion to the Wages Fund and other erroneous theories, it did not a little harm as well as good to Economic Science. Mill's most enthusiastic disciple in economics, 1833-1884 **Henry Fawcett**, went far beyond his master in his acceptance of the main doctrines of the Ricardo school. Many of the positions maintained in his "Political Economy" were abandoned by Mill before his death, particularly the Wages Fund theory; and in his "Autobiography" he traced his own progress to views which, as he said, would class him "under the general designation of Socialist." He declared himself in favour of "the common ownership in the raw material of the globe, and an equal participation of all in the benefits of combined labour." [1]

Professor Fawcett, who published his "Manual of Political Economy" in 1863, continued to

[1] "Autobiography" by John Stuart Mill (1869), pp. 232, 233.

Victorian Literature

the last to hold to the old views, and especially
to favour as little as possible the intervention
of the State. As member of Parliament, first
for Brighton and afterwards for Hackney, he
did great service by his criticisms of Indian
finance. For more than four years (1880-1884)
he held the position of Postmaster - General,
and introduced many valuable reforms into the
department under his administration. Other
economists of importance, **John Elliott Cairnes** 1824-1875
and **William Stanley Jevons**, have differed from 1835-1882
Mill in many theoretic principles; but the fairest
survey of the later developments of Mill's economics
is given by **Henry Sidgwick**, Knightbridge Pro- 1838-
fessor of Moral Philosophy at Cambridge, and by
Alfred Marshall (born 1842). In his "Principles
of Political Economy" (1883) Sidgwick attempts,
with great clearness, to criticise the conflicting
views of the older economists in the light of the
modern and more socialist views. He also attempts in his "Methods of Ethics" (1874) a compromise between the Utilitarian and the Intuitionist
schools, and he does this also in his "Elements of
Politics" (1891), a comprehensive survey of political science. Mr Marshall, who holds the Chair
of Political Economy at Cambridge, has written
"Economics of Industry" (1879), and "Principles
of Economics" (1890). A writer who did much
to make foreign economists known in England, and

who seemed at one time destined to be the able leader of a new school, was **Thomas Edward Cliffe** **1827-1882 Leslie**, whose "Essays" are full of terse and suggestive criticism. Cliffe Leslie died, however, without writing any work of first-rate importance. He did something, however, following the line of writers like Richard Jones (1790-1855), to bring academic theory to the test of actual facts.

During the last twenty years of the century, economic study has taken increasingly the direction of elaborate investigation of the circumstances of industrial life. On the one hand, a school of economic historians,—Arnold Toynbee, with a brilliant *aperçu* on "The Industrial Revolution," Thorold Rogers in his monumental "History of Agriculture and Prices," Dr Cunningham, in the "Growth of English History and Commerce," and Professor W. J. Ashley in "Economic History and Theory," have greatly extended our knowledge of past industry. On the other, we have the colossal work undertaken at his own expense by Mr Charles Booth, assisted by a group of zealous students—including H. Llewellyn Smith, D. F. Schloss, and Miss Clara Collet, now all filling official posts at the Labor Department of the Board of Trade; and Miss Beatrice Potter (now Mrs Sidney Webb) —a complete survey of London life, statistical, economic, industrial, and social. The nine volumes of this "Life and Labor of the People," already issued, constitute one of the most important statistical works ever undertaken by a private person. Mr and Mrs Sidney Webb wrote together another valuable contribution to economic science in "The History of Trade Unionism" (1894).

But political economy is merely a branch of the larger science of sociology, and for the first general treatment of the whole science, since Comte, we turn to the most characteristic philosopher of the century. **Herbert Spencer** was born at Derby, 1820- where his father was a teacher of mathematics. From his father and uncle, the latter a Congregational minister, he received his early education. Articled at seventeen years of age to a civil engineer, he followed that profession with some success for seven or eight years, when he gradually drifted into literature—a series of letters by him "On the Proper Sphere of Government" appearing in the *Nonconformist* for 1842. A few years later, he wrote for the *Westminster Review*, at the house of the editor of which magazine he met George Eliot in 1851, and began the most famous friendship of his life. It was also in 1851 that he published his first work, "Social Statics," and four years later his "Principles of Psychology." In 1861 he published his work on "Education," and the following year his "First Principles." Between that time and 1896 he has slowly built up a system of synthetic philosophy, in a dozen bulky volumes, which has secured him a very large following not only in England, but throughout the Continent and America. His "Descriptive Sociology" is the production of many writers, who have worked under his direction, collecting facts from travellers and scientists all over the world.

To have placed Psychology and Ethics on a scientific basis in harmony with the discoveries of the century is a truly great achievement. Many years have now passed away since Herbert Spencer claimed the whole domain of knowledge as his own, and undertook to revise, in accordance with the latest lights, the whole sphere of philosophy. What must have seemed intolerable presumption in 1860 became in 1896 a completed task. In universality of knowledge he rivals Aristotle and Bacon at a time when the sphere of learning is immensely larger than in their epochs. It is not within the province of this survey of literature to go through the twelve large volumes of his works in detail. We would rather point out that, to the unphilosophical reader, who would willingly know something of Spencer's literary powers, the "Study of Sociology," which he wrote for the "International Scientific Series," and the treatise on "Education" are books which all who read must enjoy.

To him, with Mill, belongs the glory of restoring to Great Britain the old supremacy in philosophy given to her by Bacon, continued by Locke, Hume, and Berkeley, but temporarily interrupted by Kant and Hegel.

Another writer who has attempted to combine psychology with physiology is **Alexander Bain, 1818-** who was for many years Professor of Logic in the University of Aberdeen, and twice Lord Rector. Bain assisted Mill in the preparation of his "Logic," and has himself written a treatise on that science, also lengthy works on "The Senses and the Intellect," and "The Emotions and the Will." Perhaps his work on "Mental and Moral Science" is his best-known contribution to student literature. Although he is the author of books on grammar and composition, Professor Bain's style is always oppressively heavy and unattractive. As Spencer and Bain combined psychology with physiology, so it was the effort of Boole and De Morgan to extend the scope of logic by an ingenious application of mathematics.

The leader for many years of the "Hegelian" school of philosophy at Oxford, which has long held the field against Mill on the one hand and Spencer on the other, was **Thomas Hill Green, who 1838-1882** was appointed Whyte Professor of Moral Philosophy in 1877, and who published the same year a series of articles in the *Contemporary Review*, on "Mr Herbert Spencer and Mr G. H. Lewes : their Application of the Doctrine of Evolution to Thought."

He was preparing for publication his "Prolegomena to Ethics" at the time of his death, and the work was finally edited by Professor A. C. Bradley, who has himself written a treatise on logic, and whose Hegelian work, entitled "Ethical Studies," is of the highest interest. Green was a moral force in Oxford, quite apart from his philosophical speculation, as the following extract from one of his lectures will indicate :—" I confess to hoping for a time when the phrase, 'the education of a gentleman,' will have lost its meaning, because the sort of education which alone makes the gentleman in any true sense will be within the reach of all. As it was the aspiration of Moses that all the Lord's people should be prophets, so with all seriousness and reverence we may hope and pray for a condition of English society in which all honest citizens will recognize themselves and be recognized by each other as gentlemen."

1817-1878   **George Henry Lewes**, whose name is frequently joined with that of Spencer by his association of biology with ethics and psychology, was the son of Charles Lee Lewes, the actor, and was one of the most versatile writers of our times. His first important work was the "Biographical History of Philosophy," originally published in 1845 in Knight's Shilling Library, but amplified without improvement into two substantial volumes in 1867. Lewes's distaste for the ordinary meta-

Victorian Literature

physics, and the severity of his criticism on Hegel, have rendered this work the *bête noir* of all transcendental students ; but it remains the one English " History of Philosophy " of any pretension. More unqualified praise may be given to the " Life of Goethe," which Lewes published in 1855. Perhaps no other man then living could have shown himself competent to deal with Goethe's many-sidedness — to discuss " Faust " and " Tasso," " Hermann und Dorothea " at one moment, the poet's biological and botanical discoveries the next, and to estimate at their true worth the speculations on colours, which Goethe held to be more calculated than his poems to secure him immortality. The book remains the standard life of the great Weimar sage in this country, and is popular in Germany, in spite of a vast Goethe literature which has been published since its appearance. In addition to these great works Lewes wrote two novels, one of which, " Ranthorpe," Charlotte Brontë praised enthusiastically. He edited the *Fortnightly Review*, and also initiated a craze for aquaria, by his " Seaside Studies ; " he endeavoured, indeed, to popularise many of the sciences, particularly physiology. His last years were devoted to philosophical questions, and his " Problems of Life and Mind " were published in fragments, the concluding volume, under George Eliot's editorship, after his death.

Sixty Years of

The earliest writer of the era to popularise
1781-1868 science was **Sir David Brewster**, an eminent
physicist, in whose *Edinburgh Cyclopædia* Carlyle
commenced his literary career. His "Life of
Newton," "Martyrs of Science," and "More
Worlds than One" are still widely read. **Michael**
1791-1867 Faraday, another famous physicist, is still better
remembered by our own generation, principally
for his popular lectures at the Royal Institution,
where he was superintendent of the laboratory for
forty-eight years. He was a blacksmith's son, and
was originally apprenticed to a bookbinder. After
his discovery of magneto - electricity, he had, he
told Tyndall, a hard struggle to decide whether he
should make wealth or science the pursuit of his
life. Tyndall calculates that Faraday could easily
have realised £150,000; but he declared for
science and died a poor man.

1820-1893 **John Tyndall**, who once said that it was his great
ambition to play the part of Schiller to this Goethe,
succeeded Faraday at the Royal Institution, and
wrote about him eloquently in his "Faraday as a
Discoverer." Tyndall was born at Leighlin
Bridge, Carlow, Ireland, in 1820. His father was
a member of the Irish constabulary. His services
to many branches of science were great; but he
concerns us here not so much by his treatises on
electricity, sound, light, and heat, or by his discoveries in diamagnetism, as by his "Lectures on

Victorian Literature

Science for Unscientific People," which, Huxley
said, was the most scientific book he had ever
read, and which has yet the transcendent merit of
giving enjoyment as well as instruction, even to the
readers of three-volume novels. In 1856 Tyndall
made a journey to Switzerland, in company with
Professor Huxley, and the friends afterwards wrote
a treatise "On the Structure and Motion of
Glaciers." Geological treatises may be said to
have given the fullest play to the literary side
of science. The work of Robert Bentley and
Sir Joseph Hooker in botany, of Michael Foster,
St George Mivart, and Francis Maitland Balfour in
biology, is, it may be, equal or superior to that
of the bulk of the writers whose achievements
we have chronicled; but it is not a part of
literature. Burdon Sanderson, Balfour Stewart,
and a host of other men, have done incalculable
service in the Victorian era — service, it is to
be feared, which scarcely obtains as generous recognition as the cheap generalisations of smaller
men ; but scientific text-books, however important,
are scarcely within the scope of these chapters.
Geology, on the other hand, is, as it were, a con-
glomerate of the sciences, and lends itself readily
to the most eloquent literary expression. Few
writers have been more widely read than **Hugh
Miller,** a Cromarty stone-mason, whose first **1802-1856**
enthusiasm for study of the rocks arose from

following his trade, but whose life was mainly devoted to journalism, and to editing *The Witness.* His "Old Red Sandstone," "Footprints of the Creator," and "The Testimony of the Rocks" were effective in kindling a taste for natural science.

The special study which Miller gave to the Red Sandstone rocks was extended by **Sir Roderick** 1792-1871 **Impey Murchison** to the Silurian System, and his work entitled "Siluria" has passed through many editions. Scotland seems to have been the nursery of geologists, for Miller and Murchison, Lyell and the brothers Geikie, were all born north of 1797-1875 the Tweed. **Sir Charles Lyell** was born at Kinnordy, in Forfarshire, and educated at Midhurst, and at Exeter College, Oxford. Called to the bar, he went the Western Circuit for two years, but, when attending some of Dr Buckland's lectures, he became attached to geology. His "Principles of Geology," first published in 1830, caused a revolution in the science. Never before had there been presented such a connected illustration of the influences which had caused the earth's changes in the unresting distribution of land and water areas. Much of Lyell's great work reads like a fairy tale ; much might have been thought the fruit of an imaginative rather than of a scientific mind. Lyell's smaller book, the "Student's Elements of Geology," was injured in

Victorian Literature

literary merit by the progressive study of the science of which he had been the second father. The constant addition of fresh knowledge, and his conversion to Darwin's views, necessitated the continual rewriting of parts and further revision by other hands after the author's death. "The Antiquity of Man" (in defence of Darwin's theory) is of more value from a literary standpoint. Before the beginning of the reign **William Buckland**, Dean 1784-1856 of Westminster, by whose lectures Lyell had so much profited, had written his famous Bridgewater Treatise on "Geology and Mineralogy considered with reference to Natural Theology." His son, **Frank Buckland**, wrote clever and readable books 1826-1880 on "Natural History," and had genuine enthusiasm for the study of animal life; but he was charged with having vulgarised the studies in which he took so keen an interest. The most distinguished living geologist is Sir Archibald Geikie, who is now director-general of the Geological Survey of the United Kingdom. His "Text Book," which was first published in 1882, is a model of lucid writing, and his essays are among the most pleasant literary products of the age. His brother, James Geikie, has written an important work on glaciation, entitled "The Great Ice Age."

But the scientific literature of the past sixty years might almost be said to be summarised in the work of **Charles Darwin**. A funeral in Westminster 1809-1882

Abbey, amid the mourning of many nations, closed the career of one whose life-work had often been greeted with scorn. "Our century is Darwin's century," said a leading German newspaper (*Allgemeine Zeitung*) at his death, and the statement is no exaggeration. Those who witnessed the long stream of prelates and nobles who filed through the Abbey at his funeral, the then Archbishop of Canterbury (Dr Tait) and the present Prime Minister (Lord Salisbury) among the number, could not but recall the reception of the great investigator's theory twenty years before. Bishop Wilberforce in particular denounced it in the *Quarterly Review* as "a flimsy speculation." Darwin's antecedents were of a nature such as, on the principle of heredity, a great man should possess. His paternal grandfather, Erasmus Darwin, was a poet, whose "Botanic Garden" may still be read with interest. His maternal grandfather was Josiah Wedgwood, the famous potter. Darwin was the son of a doctor of Shrewsbury, and was educated at the Grammar School of that city and at Christ's College, Cambridge. Here his natural history studies were sympathetically directed by Professor Henslow, the botanist, by whose recommendation he was selected to accompany the *Beagle* on its expedition to survey the South American coast. The results of his travels were embodied in his first important work, "Journals of

Victorian Literature

Researches during a Voyage round the World," which was published in 1839, and was republished under the title of " A Naturalist's Voyage round the World." In the same year he married his cousin, Miss Wedgwood, and, after a few years of London life, took up his residence in a pleasant country house at Down, near Beckenham in Kent. Here he pursued his remarkable investigations until his death, surrounded by his accomplished children, and finding, as he told a friend, his highest emotional gratification in the joys of family life and a love of animate nature. Two of his sons, George Howard Darwin and Francis Darwin, have done good work in science, the one in geology and astronomy, the other in botany. Darwin himself wrote also on the "Structure and Distribution of Coral Reefs," revolutionising the popular view concerning these remarkable phenomena. Discovering that reef-building polyps cannot live at depths of more than twenty fathoms, he found it necessary to explain the presence of rocks built by them which rise from more than 2000 feet below the surface of the sea. This he did on the hypothesis of a gradual subsidence of the sea-floor whilst the polyps are at work. This view has since been generally accepted by geologists, although somewhat modified by Dr John Murray's observation in the *Challenger* expedition, that the reefs are not always of solid coral, and that they may in

many cases have been formed on the cones of
extinct volcanoes.

Darwin had pondered for many years over the
theory which was to make him famous before he
decided to bring his conclusions before the public.
After considerable observation of every form of
animal and vegetable life and experiments in
selective breeding he concluded that the species
of plants and animals now on the earth were
not created in their present form, but had been
evolved by unbroken descent with modification
of structure from cruder forms, the remains of
many of which are constantly discovered in
the older rocks.   He discovered in 1858 that
1822-   **Alfred Russel Wallace** had independently
arrived at the same conclusions, and so it
was agreed that their views should be jointly laid
before the Linnæan Society.   In 1859 the "Origin
of Species" was published, and it was followed by
a number of works bearing upon the same subject,
the most notable of all being the "Descent of
Man." Darwin's work on "Earth Worms," perhaps
the most purely literary of all his writings, appeared
the year before his death.   It is not the province
of a sketch of Victorian literature to discuss the
many important bearings of the Darwinian hypothesis.   Received with unbounded contempt by
literary men so eminent as Carlyle and Ruskin, it
was accepted only with qualification by men of

science like Agassiz, Carpenter, and Owen ; but an overwhelming majority of scientific men in England, America, and above all in Continental countries, have declared in its favour. The theory has received popular interpretation in Germany from Haeckel, and in England from Huxley, although in this connection we must not forget **George John Romanes**, the author of "Animal Intelligence" and 1848-1894 "Mental Evolution in Animals," Grant Allen, and Edward Clodd.

Thomas Henry Huxley, one of the greatest of 1825-1895 our men of science, was of interest not only on account of his vast scientific attainments, but for his profound acquaintance with metaphysics, as illustrated in his "Life of Hume," his wide culture, and his exquisite literary style. He was born and educated at Ealing, in Middlesex, where his father was a schoolmaster. He studied medicine at the Charing Cross Hospital, then entered the Royal Navy as an assistant surgeon, and went in the *Rattlesnake* to survey the Barrier Reef of Australia. The papers which he sent to the Royal and Linnæan Societies gave him fame. After his return he devoted himself to original research ; but work of that sort brings no recompense in money, and Huxley's means were narrow. In 1854, however, he obtained the chairs of Natural History and Palæontology at the School of Mines, and to this he afterwards added the appointment of

Inspector of Fisheries. The "blue ribbon" of science, the Presidency of the Royal Society, was conferred on him in 1883. Huxley wrote much on biological problems, and by the publication of his "Physiography" gave a new name to the science which has extended the scope of the old Physical Geography : but his chief interest for us here is in his "Lay Sermons," "Addresses and Reviews," his "Critiques and Addresses," and his "American Addresses," all of which may take rank among the finest prose of our age.

As an interesting contrast to the work of Darwin and Huxley, and all that it has implied to modern literature, one may refer once again to the movement inspired by Cardinal Newman. His most prominent associates for many years, neither of whom, however, left the Church of England for the Church of Rome, were Pusey and Keble.

1800-1882 **Edward Bouverie Pusey** was practically the founder of the modern High Church movement in the Anglican community. A writer of "Tracts for the Times," he was, after Newman had "gone over to Rome," the recognized head of the movement, and his followers were frequently called "Puseyites." A demoralization of the party seemed inevitable on Newman's secession, but the publication of Dr Pusey's "Letter to Keble" gave it fresh life. In 1866 his "Eirenicon," a

Victorian Literature

proposal for the reunion of Christendom, drew a reply from Cardinal Newman, with whom, however, he maintained the profoundest friendship to the end. **John Keble**, who was born at Fairford, 1792-1866 in Gloucestershire, was a man of far higher gifts. Educated at Corpus Christi College, Oxford, he obtained a fellowship at Oriel. For some years he was Professor of Poetry at Oxford, a position for which he had qualified himself by the publication of the "Christian Year," a volume of religious poems for every Sunday and church festival, many of which have been admitted into the hymnology of all the Christian sects. Perhaps truer poetry is to be found in his "Lyra Innocentium," a series of poems on children, for there the human element is more marked. Keble also wrote a "Life of Bishop Wilson," and published several volumes of sermons.

The movement of Liberal theology, to which men like Keble gave the name of "national apostasy," was headed in its earlier developments by Archbishop Whately and Dr Arnold of Rugby, and more recently by the Rev. Frederick Denison Maurice and Dean Stanley. **Richard Whately**, 1787-1863 who was at Oriel with Keble, had published his once popular "Logic" and "Rhetoric" before the commencement of the reign of Victoria, and in 1831 had been made Archbishop of Dublin,

a position which he held till his death, in 1863,
winning all hearts by his kindness and liberality,
by his generous tolerance and zeal for progress.
His "Logic" is chiefly of importance for the
impetus it gave to the study of that science.
His "Christian Evidences" gained in its day a
1795-1842 wider audience. **Thomas Arnold** was born at
East Cowes, in the Isle of Wight, and was educated at Winchester, and with Keble at Corpus
Christi College, Oxford. After ordination he removed to Laleham-on-Thames, where he prepared
young men for the universities. When, in 1827,
the head-mastership of Rugby became vacant,
Arnold was elected on the strength of a recommendation by Dr Hawkins, to the effect that he
"would change the face of education all through
the public schools of England." The prophecy
was fulfilled. He was the first to introduce
modern languages and modern history and mathematics into the regular school course. At the
same time he always insisted on the value of the
classics as a basis of education, and himself prepared an edition of "Thucydides," and wrote a
"History of Rome" in its earlier periods, which is
at least eminently interesting. His services to his
country as an educational reformer were even
greater on the moral side. Dr Arnold was a
purifying influence to men of the higher classes,
to a degree which is inexplicable to the present

generation. For a time he was unpopular, and his school suffered, through his advocacy of church reform and his association with political Liberalism ; but the success of his pupils at the universities had caused a reaction in his favour at the time of his death, which occurred all too early, for he was only forty-seven. Of his many distinguished pupils, perhaps the best known are Tom Hughes and Dean Stanley. **Thomas Hughes,** who in 1882 1823-1896 was made a county-court judge, wrote many books, but only one of them entitles him to be remembered to-day. In a moment of happy inspiration, he wrote the finest boy's book in the language. "Tom Brown's School Days" was published in 1857. It is a picture of life at Rugby, under Dr Arnold's healthy, manly guidance.

Arthur Penrhyn Stanley wrote his "Life of 1815-1881 Dr Arnold" in 1844. A son of Edward Stanley, Bishop of Norwich, he was born at Alderley, in Cheshire. From Rugby he went to Balliol College, Oxford, where he had an exceptionally distinguished career. In 1851 he became a canon of Canterbury, and his picturesque "Memorials of Canterbury" were the outcome of residence in that city. In 1863 he was made Dean of Westminster, notwithstanding the opposition of the High Church party, to whom the theological views expressed in his numerous works were distasteful. Of these writings, "Sinai and Palestine," "Lectures on the Eastern Church," and "Lectures on the Jewish Church," are the best known. As Dean of Westminster Dr Stanley became an active leader of the Broad Church movement. Although not a contributor to "Essays and Reviews" his services to the movement were incalculable. He invited Max Müller to lecture in the Abbey, befriended Père Hyacinthe, and gave sympathy to Bishop Colenso. His speeches in the Lower House of Convocation, particularly one in which he proposed the suppression of the Athanasian Creed in the services of the Church, made him many enemies; but few ecclesiastics have been so beloved by both sovereign and people. One recalls the pleasant, active little man, so proud of his Abbey Church, with a deep sigh that he should be no more. His life was written by his successor, Dean Bradley.

Of the contributors to "Essays and Reviews," the manifesto of the Broad Church party, which appeared in 1860, Frederick Temple must be mentioned, because his contribution, "The Education of the World," led to a frantic effort to prevent his receiving the bishopric of Exeter, an effort which was unsuccessful. In 1885 Dr Temple was made Bishop of London, and in 1896 Archbishop of Canterbury. Other distinguished writers in "Essays and Reviews" were Dr Jowett and Mr 1817-1893 Mark Pattison. **Benjamin Jowett**, master of

Victorian Literature

Balliol, who wrote the essay on "The Interpretation of Scripture," achieved his greatest successes by his brilliant translations of Plato, Thucydides, and "The Politics" of Aristotle. His Plato drew from John Bright, who was little inclined to appreciate the great thoughts of the Athenian philosopher, an expression of admiration for the classic English of the Oxford professor. Jowett's life was written by Evelyn Abbott and Lewis Campbell. **Mark Pattison**, whose contribution 1813-1884 to "Essays and Reviews" was on "The Tendencies of Religious Thought in England," assisted Newman and Pusey in the early days of the Tractarian movement, but finally went over to the Liberalism which they so much dreaded. In 1861 he was elected Rector of Lincoln College, Oxford. Pattison was a profound scholar. Few men have led lives so absorbed in books. The results of his learning are apparent in his interesting "Life of Isaac Casaubon," which he had hoped to follow by a life of Scaliger.

But men like Jowett and Pattison have been the arm-chair representatives of a movement which found one of its most active supporters in **John Frederick Denison Maurice**. Maurice was the son 1805-1872 of a Unitarian minister, and was born at Normanstone, near Lowestoft. For a time he was editor of the *Athenæum*, but joined the Anglican Church in 1831, and accepted a curacy near

Leamington. A treatise entitled "Subscription no Bondage," which defined his position in the Church, excited much attention, as did also his tracts on the "Kingdom of Christ." In conjunction with Kingsley and Hughes he published pamphlets called "Politics for the People," and organised the Christian socialist and co-operative movement of 1850. Like Kingsley, Maurice may be labelled a Broad Churchman, not so much on doctrinal grounds as for the breadth of his sympathies. It was social rather than theological problems to which he attached importance. Kingsley, indeed, described himself to correspondents as a Broad Churchman, a High Churchman, and an Evangelical, as the mood seemed to take him. Bishop Colenso is a good type of the more

1814-1883 militant theologians. **John William Colenso** first came before the public as the author of mathematical text-books. At this time he was vicar of Forncett St Mary, in Norfolk, but in 1853 he was made Bishop of Natal. In South Africa he was a zealous advocate of the rights of the natives against the oppression of the Boers and Cape Town officials; but in a measure his influence was weakened by the publication of his work on Biblical criticism, "The Pentateuch and Book of Joshua Critically Examined," which was condemned by both Houses of Convocation as heretical. When Colenso came to England in 1874 he was inhibited from preaching in the dioceses of London, Lincoln, and Oxford. At Oxford, however, his sermon was read from the pulpit of Balliol while the Bishop sat below, and the same device was pursued at Mr Stopford Brooke's Church in London. Dean Stanley invited him to the Abbey pulpit, claiming freedom from the jurisdiction of Dr Jackson, the then Bishop of London ; but Colenso declined to increase the ill-feeling which had been excited.

Another distinguished member of the Broad Church party, **Edwin Abbott**, was head-master of **1838-** the City of London School from 1865 to 1889. He has published several educational works. His religious influence has developed itself through "Philochristus ; Memoirs of a Disciple of our Lord," and "Onesimus ; Memoirs of a Disciple of St Paul," also by a volume of sermons, "Through Nature to Christ," which is perhaps the best evidence of the development of the Broad Church movement. Dr Whately, one of its founders, argued for the miracles as indicative of the Divine origin of Christianity ; Dr Abbott esteems the insistence on miracles as a bar to belief. Perhaps the purest and most inspiring of all the eloquent teachers belonging to this party was **Frederick William Robertson** of Brighton, **1816-1853** whose sermons have been widely read, especially in America, and whose lectures are as helpful and bracing as any written in our time. Robertson's remarkable career of only thirty-seven years has been made known to us by the beautiful life which was written by Mr Stopford Brooke. **Stopford** **1832-** **Augustus Brooke** was born in Dublin and educated at Trinity College. At first he was a Church of England clergyman and a Queen's Chaplain, but seceded in 1880 on account of his inability to believe in many supernatural phases of Christian teaching. His "Primer of English Literature," "History of Early English Poetry," "Theology in the English Poets," and "Life of Milton" have the ring of the genuine, and, indeed, of the great, critic.

Outside the pale of the Anglican community, but powerful factors in that same Broad Church movement which has been charged with "stretching the old formula to meet the new facts," one recalls the names of Lynch and Martineau. **1818-1871 Thomas Toke Lynch** was born at Dunmow, in Essex, and held for many years the ministry of a small Congregational Church, first in Grafton Street and afterwards in the Hampstead Road, London. He died in comparative obscurity; but the poems in his "Rivulet," once condemned as heretical, have found their way into most hymnologies.

1805- **James Martineau** was born at Norwich, and was originally educated for the profession of civil engineer, but turned to theological studies, and was for some time the minister of a Presbyterian

Church in Dublin. Then, during a residence in Liverpool, he became a supporter of the philosophy of Bentham and the elder Mill, but finally abandoned that position for Kantian metaphysics. Thenceforth he was to be a great power on behalf of the Theistic and Unitarian position, and he turned vigorously upon the materialistic beliefs which he had abandoned, and was, it may be added, somewhat too harsh to his sister Harriet when, later in life, she adopted them. His "Endeavour after the Christian Life" and "Hours of Thought on Sacred Things" are two of his best known works, although a more philosophical interest attaches to his "Study of Spinoza" and his "Types of Ethical Theory."

I have dwelt at some length on the work of the High Church and Broad Church parties during the reign, because with these bodies it has been a period of great literary achievement, and it can scarcely be claimed that Evangelicanism, however earnest, zealous, and numerically powerful, has added much of enduring worth to religious literature. **Richard William Church**, Dean of St Paul's, 1815-1890 who wrote so eloquently on Dante and St Anselm, belonged to the Liberal High Church school, as did also **Henry Parry Liddon**, a canon of the same 1829-1890 cathedral, whose Bampton lectures "On the Divinity of Jesus Christ" marked him out as one of the most eloquent of modern preachers. One of the greatest scholars in the English Church, **Joseph Barber Lightfoot**, Bishop of Durham, who replied to the author of "Supernatural Religion" belonged to the same party. Midway between the Broad Church and the Evangelical schools we find **Frederick William Farrar**, Dean of Canterbury, who, as head-master of Marlborough College, wrote stories of boy life. He succeeded Kingsley as a Canon of Westminster, and excited much attention by his sermons on the doctrine of eternal punishment. His lives of Christ and of St Paul have been widely read. **John Charles Ryle**, Bishop of Liverpool, has been perhaps the most famous literary exponent of the Evangelical position. "Shall we know one another in Heaven" and "Bible Inspiration" were characteristic books from his pen. **John Saul Howson**, Dean of Chester, who, in conjunction with the Rev. W. J. Conybeare, wrote an able work on "The Life and Epistles of St Paul," was also a Low Churchman.

The most distinguished Nonconformist minister of the Victorian period, and the man whose sermons found most readers, was **Charles Haddon Spurgeon**, with whom eloquence and earnestness were combined with the possession of a simple English style, which he derived from a study of the Puritan fathers. In "John Ploughman's Talk" (1868) Spurgeon put forth

1828-1889

1831-

1816-

1816-1885

1834-1892

much homely wisdom in a quaint and humorous garb.

I have said well nigh enough concerning speculative writers and theologians, but it is necessary to mention here **Henry Longueville Mansel,** who succeeded Milman as Dean of St 1820-1871 Paul's. Mansel was a vigorous defender of the Anglican position. "The Limits of Religious Thought" was the title of one of his books; "Metaphysics, or the Philosophy of Consciousness, Phenomenal and Real" was another, but he crossed swords with many disputants, with F. D. Maurice, with J. S. Mill, and indeed he was ever a fighter, subtle and skilful. Another theologian, **Cardinal Manning,** was a disputant on behalf of 1808-1892 Roman Catholicism, he having left the Anglican Church in 1851. His many books and sermons are to-day only of interest to the theological student. His life was written in 1896, and caused much controversy through its exceeding candour and indiscretion.

Philosophy has had notable students also in Ferrier, Caird, and Clifford. **James Frederick Ferrier** who was a nephew of Susan Ferrier the 1808-1864 author of "Marriage," was professor of moral philosophy at St Andrews. He wrote "Lectures in Greek Philosophy" and other works. **Edward**

1835-   **Caird** is master of Balliol and he has written
         "Philosophy of Kant," "Essays on Literature
         and Philosophy," and "The Evolution of
1845-1879 Religion." **William Kingdon Clifford** belonged
         to the opposite camp. He obtained an early
         reputation as a mathematician and became
         professor of applied mathematics in University
         College, London, in 1871. His powerful con-
         tributions to the literary side of science were
         contained in "Seeing and Thinking" and
         "Lectures and Essays," the latter volume being
         edited after his death by his friends Mr Leslie
         Stephen and Sir Frederick Pollock.

         The three most notable books that we have
         seen from the anti-theological side, apart from
         Matthew Arnold's "Literature and Dogma," are
         "The Creed of Christendom," "Phases of Faith,"
         and "Supernatural Religion," although to these
         may perhaps be added translations of the Lives of
         Christ, of Strauss, and of Renan. The "Creed of
         Christendom" was the work of **William Rathbone**
1809-1881 **Greg,** who wrote also "Enigmas of Life" (1872),
         and "Rocks Ahead" (1874). "Phases of Faith"
1805-1897 was the work of **Francis William Newman,** a
         younger brother of Cardinal Newman, but at the
         opposite pole of religious conviction. He has
         written many books, the most successful being one
         on "The Soul" (1849). Another on "Theism"

(1858), was inspired by the same theistic, but non-Christian impulse. " Phases of Faith (1858), was his most successful work. The author of " Supernatural Religion" is Walter Richard Cassels, who has also published a reply to Bishop Lightfoot's strictures upon his larger work—a work now all but forgotten, but which created a considerable sensation at the time of its appearance.

The age has been, particularly in its later developments, an age of good critics of literature. Criticism unhappily rarely lasts much beyond its own decade. Even Mr Matthew Arnold lives now only by his poetry, and the many good things that he said about books are being steadily forgotten. Arnold was a great critic, and so also was **Walter Pater,** whose " Marius the Epicurean " **1839-1894** and " Imaginary Portraits " should have ranked him with writers of imagination were it not that criticism was his dominant faculty. Pater has been described as "the most rhythmical of English prose writers," and his " Renaissance : Studies in Art and Poetry," and his " Appreciations " give him a very high place among the writers of our time.

Philip Gilbert Hamerton was another great **1834-1894** critic, who wrote at least one work of imagination. " Marmorne " is a very pretty story of life in France. With every aspect of French life Mr

Hamerton was well acquainted, as he lived in that country for very many years. He wrote regularly upon art topics, and edited an art magazine, *The Portfolio;* but it is by his volume of essays entitled "The Intellectual Life" that he will be most kindly remembered for many a year to come.

Certain writers whom I must mention are entitled to a place both as critics and as poets. Mr W. E. Henley, Mr F. W. H. Myers, William Bell Scott, and William Allingham for 1849- example. **William Ernest Henley** has written plays in conjunction with R. L. Stevenson, and his "Book of Verses" and "Song of the Sword" entitle him to very high rank among the poets of the day. But he is also a critic of exceptional vigour and force, and since Matthew Arnold there has been no volume of criticism so full of discrimination and sound judgment as "Views and Reviews." Ill health has compelled Mr Henley to waste much of his undoubted talent. He is at present editing fine library editions of Burns 1843- and Byron. **Frederic William Henry Myers** wrote "Saint Paul," a poem of considerable reputation, but his critical essays are more widely known. They were published in two volumes, "Classical" and "Modern," and are full of delightful ideas delightfully expressed. His biography of Wordsworth is a daintily fanciful memoir, abound-

ing in good criticism. Mr Myers's brother Ernest
is also a poet, and so also was **William Bell Scott.** 1811-1890
He was, it is true, a poet of a narrow range,
but a critic of great energy and industry. Bell
Scott became best known by his "Autobiography,"
published after his death. In it he discussed
Rossetti and the Pre-Raphaelite movement with
sufficient frankness. **William Allingham** wrote 1824-1889
many poems and ballads full of the Celtic spirit,
and of Ireland, which he loved as the land of his
birth. Allingham was for a time editor of *Fraser's
Magazine*, and he contributed regularly to the chief
literary periodicals of his day.

Literary critics of importance to-day are Edward
Dowden, Richard Garnett, George Saintsbury,
Edmund Gosse, Leslie Stephen, and Andrew Lang
—all of whom are happily living and writing.

Edward Dowden, who is an Irishman, and a 1843-
professor of Trinity College, Dublin, has a genius
for accuracy and is a master of detail. For textual
criticism of Wordsworth and Shelley he has no
superior. He has an immense knowledge of the
literature of many languages, and holds without
dispute the first place among living students of
German literature in this country. His knowledge
of English literature is profound, and in "Shakspere, his Mind and Art," and "Studies in Literature," he has said some singularly illuminating

things about books. With his "Life of Shelley"
one observes a certain deterioration; Professor
Dowden, with all his profound love of literature,
has scarcely the qualities which would find attraction in the curiously impulsive character of the
poet Shelley. Dowden was happier when writing
about Southey, and he is still more at home with
great impersonal literary figures like Shakspere
and Goethe.

1835- **Richard Garnett,**—better known to the world
to-day as Dr Garnett—has also written on Shelley,
not merely with sympathy but with partisanship.
Dr Garnett, who is honourably associated with
the British Museum Library, is a most acute critic,
a biographer of Carlyle and Emerson, a translator
from the Greek and German, and, like Professor
Dowden, a poet.

1845- **George Saintsbury,** who is Professor of English
Literature at the University of Edinburgh, has been
an industrious critic for many years, and his knowledge of French literature in particular is profound.
His acquaintance with English literature in the
seventeenth century has, however, considerably
vitiated his style. It is not easy to tolerate the
phraseology of the seventeenth century in modern
books. This defect of style is regrettably noticeable in two volumes of literary history which Pro-

Victorian Literature

fessor Saintsbury has published, one dealing with the seventeenth and the other with the nineteenth century. It is in certain brief biographies of Sir Walter Scott and others that Professor Saintsbury is most excellent; but his wide knowledge and his genuine grasp of the most salient characteristics of good literature are indisputable qualities which rank him high among the bookmen of his day.

Edmund Gosse is not less distinguished than the 1849-writers I have named. He would be widely known as a writer of charming verse were he not actively engaged in literary criticism. The son of a famous naturalist, Mr Gosse is the author of many admirably written books about the literature of the past and the present. What Carlyle so largely did for German literature by introducing it to English readers Mr Gosse has done for Scandinavian literature. In conjunction with Mr William Archer—a dramatic critic of singular insight—he has translated Ibsen, whose influence has been as marked during the past ten years as the influence of German writers was marked during the previous thirty. Mr Gosse's best biography is his "Life of Gray."

A critic of remarkable learning is **Leslie Stephen,** 1832-whose " Hours in a Library " and " History of English Thought in the Eighteenth Century " are books which have profoundly impressed the age. Mr Leslie Stephen has written a large number of biographies, all of them characterised by singular accuracy, by remarkable graces of style, and by genuine insight. He was the first editor of the *Dictionary of National Biography*, a work which has proved invaluable to students of our later literature.

1844-   **Andrew Lang** is the last of the critics I have named, and not the least active. He has shone in many branches of literary work. His " Ballads and Lyrics of Old France," "Ballades in Blue China," and numerous other verses, have gained him considerable reputation as a poet. His translations of Homer and Theocritus are by many counted the finest translations that our literature has seen. Some have contended that his musical prose rendering of the Odyssey is incomparably superior to all the efforts of Pope, of Cowper, and of the many other poets who have attempted to render Homer in verse. Mr Lang is an authority on folk-lore; he has joined issue with Professor Max Müller on many points which are of keen interest to those who are attracted towards the science of language and the study of comparative religion. As a writer of fairy-tales, and as the editor of books of fairy-stories, Mr Lang has endeared himself to thousands belonging to the younger generation. But all this is but dimly and inefficiently to appraise Mr Lang's marvellous versatility. He has written fiction, history, and, above all, biography, his biographical work including a Life of Sir Stafford Northcote and a Life of John Gibson Lockhart, Scott's son-in-law.

Biography has generally been written by literary critics, and one requires no apology in any case for ranking the biographers among the critics. **John Gibson Lockhart** himself was a 1794-1854 notable example. He was editor of the *Quarterly Review*, and an industrious writer for many years ; but he is best known to us by his "Life of Sir Walter Scott," which was published—it is worthy of note—in 1837, the year of the Queen's accession. Lockhart's "Scott" is beyond question the most important biography of the reign. The longest is that of Milton by Professor Masson. **David Masson** has held a chair of literature in 1822- University College, London, and later at Edinburgh. Few men know English literature better than he. His name will always be associated with his monumental Life of Milton, a solid, accurate, exhaustive book ; but he has written pleasantly on "British Novelists and their Styles" and "Drummond of Hawthornden," besides sundry other books. Many of our poets have had capable

M   177

biographers. Professor Knight of St Andrews has
devoted himself for many years to Wordsworth,
and has written his biography besides editing
his collected works. The late James Dykes
Campbell (1835-1894) wrote a biography of
Coleridge distinguished by remarkable thoroughness. Professor W. J. Courthope has proved
himself Pope's best biographer and editor, and is
giving us a good "History of English Poetry,"
which at present reaches only to the Reformation.
Mr Churton Collins, one of the most thorough of
our critics, has written on Swift, as has also Sir
Henry Craik; and Swift's life in Ireland has been
gracefully sketched by Mr Richard Ashe King, a
novelist whose "Love the Debt" and "The Wear-
ing of the Green" have commanded a large audience. Swift has been a favourite subject with the
biographers. A life of him was the task upon which
1812-1876 John Forster was engaged at the time of his death.
Forster was an untiring biographer, and he bene-
fited literature as well by his death as by his life, in
that he bequeathed his fine library of books and
manuscripts to the nation. John Forster wrote a
Life of Walter Savage Landor, another of Goldsmith, and another of Charles Dickens, against
which it was urged that he had introduced too
much of his own personality. Perhaps Forster's
best work was his "Life of Sir John Eliot," an
expansion of a biography of that patriot which he

had contributed to his " Statesmen of the Common-wealth."

Biography is the great medium of instruction and inspiration of that little band of Positive philosophers who accept their gospel from Auguste Comte, whose " Philosophie Positive" they have translated into English. " Study the 'Philosophie Positive' for yourself," says George Henry Lewes, who, with George Eliot, had much enthusiasm for the new cult ; " study it patiently, give it the time and thought you would not grudge to a new science or a new language ; and then, whether you accept or reject the system, you will find your mental horizon irrevocably enlarged. ' But six stout volumes !' exclaims the hesitating aspirant : Well, yes ; six volumes requiring to be meditated as well as read. I admit that they 'give pause' in this busy bustling life of ours ; but if you reflect how willingly six separate volumes of philosophy would be read in the course of the year the undertaking seems less formidable. No one who considers the immense importance of a doctrine which will give unity to his life, would hesitate to pay a higher price than that of a year's study." Among the most gifted of the Positivists is **Frederic Harrison**, whose " Order and Progress," 1831-and " Choice of Books," are well known. Among his companions in literary and religious warfare

1831-1888 have been **James Cotter Morison**, who wrote biographies of St Bernard of Clairvaux and Macaulay, "The Service of Man" which was a contribution to religious propaganda; and Richard Congreve (born 1818), who was a pupil of Dr Arnold at Rugby, and who has written many thoughtful political tracts.

An attempt to popularise Comte by an abridgment of his great work was made by **Harriet** 1802-1876 **Martineau**, who was born at Norwich, and was one of the most versatile of Victorian writers. None of her work has stood the test of time, perhaps because she had so little of real genius, although possessed undoubtedly of great intellectual endowments. Not the less readily should we recognise that she exercised considerable influence upon her own generation. She wrote many stories dealing with social subjects, and tales illustrative of Political Economy, which dispersed many a popular illusion. In a visit to America she learned to sympathise with the Northern States, and perhaps no writer of the day did so much in England to excite sympathy with the cause which ultimately proved victorious. Miss Martineau's "Biographical Sketches" were originally published in the *Daily News*, a journal to which she was for many years a regular contributor, and for which she wrote her own obituary notice. Her historical work is mere compilation, destitute alike of originality and thoroughness, and the greater part of her other work has proved to be ephemeral. Such tales, however, as "Deerbrook" and "The Hour and the Man" have still admiring readers. The publication of her "Letters on the Laws of Man's Nature and Development" (1851) excited much controversy, although her fearless honesty won the respect even of her opponents.

A writer who distinguished himself most notably at one period by a combination of antagonism to Supernatural Christianity, and a gift for writing biography, was **John Morley**. Mr Morley was 1838-born at Blackburn, and educated at Cheltenham and at Lincoln College, Oxford. Much of his work was done in journalism; he edited in succession the *Morning Star*, the *Literary Gazette*, the *Fortnightly Review*, the *Pall Mall Gazette*, and *Macmillan's Magazine*. He resigned the editorship of the *Pall Mall Gazette* in 1883, when he entered Parliament as member for Newcastle-on-Tyne, and he gave up his post on *Macmillan's Magazine* on entering a Liberal Cabinet in 1886. He still edits the "English Men of Letters Series," a remarkable collection of handy biographies, for which he wrote a "Life of Burke." His literary achievement, apart from his essays, is entirely biographical, but it was of enormous influence upon the intellectual development of thoughtful young men at the

Universities during the seventies and eighties. He has written lives of Voltaire, Rousseau, and Diderot, which throw much light on the period prior to the French Revolution, and give abundant evidence that, had he not devoted himself to politics he would have been able to produce a history of the French Revolution of inestimable value. On the other hand his "Life of Cobden" was a failure from a literary standpoint. The essay "On Compromise" is a most interesting development of the fundamental idea of Milton's "Areopagitica," and is probably the most exhaustive treatment of the question—how far we are justified in keeping back the expression of our opinions in deference to the views and customs of our fellow-men.

Another good biographer who gave up to Parliament time which might have been better employed, from the point of view of a lover of letters, **1838-** is **Sir George Otto Trevelyan**, whose life of his uncle, Lord Macaulay, is a delightful biography, full of entertainment for the most frivolous of readers. Not less entertaining is Sir George Trevelyan's "Early History of Charles James Fox" (1880), a book which makes one wish that the writer had devoted himself to that epoch of our history, and had done for the period of the Georges what his uncle had done for their immediate predecessors.

Victorian Literature

Lord Houghton wrote poetry as Richard 1809-1885
Monckton Milnes, and his lines are still fre-
quently quoted. But his biography of Keats—
" Life, Letters, and Literary Remains of John
Keats (1848)," although not now in any publisher's
list, is certain to be long remembered. Lord
Houghton's life was written by his friend, Sir
Wemyss Reid, author also of a " Monograph on
Charlotte Brontë." His son, after serving as Lord-
Lieutenant of Ireland, became Earl of Crewe ; his
daughter, Florence Henniker, keeps alive the
literary tradition of the family, and is known as a
writer of short stories. Lord Houghton had a
genuine love of letters and of the society of literary
men. So also had **Henry Crabb Robinson**, whose 1775-1867
diary edited by Dr Sadler (1869) brings one in
touch with all the literary men and women of the
period. At his house in Russell Square Robinson
gave breakfasts, to which it became a distinction
to be invited. **Samuel Rogers's** breakfasts have 1763-1855
been described in many memoirs. Rogers wrote
all his poems long years before the Queen began
to reign, but he lived for another thirty years with
the reputation of a good conversationalist and
story-teller. His " Table Talk " was published in
1856, and it is full of good stories. Two valuable books concerning Rogers have been written
by Mr Peter William Clayden, " Early Life of

183

Samuel Rogers," and "Rogers and His Contemporaries."

An important biography was written by **James Spedding**, whose whole life was devoted to a study of Bacon, and to a thorough destruction of Macaulay's criticism upon the great philosopher. The "Letters and the Life of Francis Bacon, including all his Occasional Works, newly collected and set forth, with a Commentary Biographical and Historical," was published in seven volumes between 1857 and 1874.

1810-1881

Two of the most notable political philosophers of the era were George Cornewall Lewis and Bagehot. **Sir George Lewis** held important posts in the Governments of his day, being at one time Home Secretary and at another Secretary of State for War. He wrote "A Dialogue on the Best Form of Government" and many other treatises. **Walter Bagehot** was one of the greatest authorities of his day on banking and finance. He wrote "Physics and Politics," "Economic Studies," and several other works which have little relation to literature; but his "Literary Studies" indicated a critical acquaintance with the best books. A brilliant publicist of our day, who combines, like Bagehot, a love of affairs with keen literary instincts, is

1806-1863

1826-1877

Victorian Literature

Goldwin Smith, who has made his home in 1823-
Toronto, Canada, for many years now, but who
was once intimately associated with Oxford University. Goldwin Smith has written many books
and pamphlets, one on " The Relations between
England and America," another on " The Political
Destiny of Canada," and he has written a short
biography of Cowper.

The most famous traveller of the reign and one
of our greatest men of letters was **George Borrow**, 1803-1881
who went to Spain as an agent of the British
and Foreign Bible Society. Hence his " Bible in
Spain," which has become one of the most popular
books in our language as it is one of the most
fascinating. It was first published in 1843 under
the title " The Bible in Spain, or Journeys,
Adventures, and Imprisonments of an Englishman in an attempt to circulate the Scriptures in
the Peninsula." "Lavengro" (1851) and "The
Romany Rye" (1857) have enjoyed almost an
equal popularity with " The Bible in Spain."

Herman Melville (1819-1891) was an American citizen, and his work, therefore, does not
come within the scope of this volume. I am the
more sorry for this, that I consider Melville's
name is entitled to rank with that of George
Borrow as one of the two travellers during the

epoch whose books make literature. It is small disparagement to the majority of our great travellers that they have not been men of letters, that their books, although serviceable to their generation, are of little moment considered from the standpoint of art. Although Mr H. M. Stanley, Dr Nansen, and other adventurous spirits of our time, may be quite as important in the general drift of the world's doings as any of the literary men whose names are contained in this volume, their books have no place whatever in literature. It is noteworthy, however, that books written by travellers have been, during the past ten years or more, by far the most popular form of reading, apart from fiction. Interest in historical study and speculative writing seems to have declined ; interest in travel is as marked as ever.

The journalism of the reign has been so intimately associated with literature that were my space more ample I should have chosen to devote a chapter to that subject alone. Many of the men I have mentioned, perhaps most of them, have at one time or another contributed to the journals or magazines of the day. Even the novelists have a peculiar interest in journalism, because of late years as large a proportion of their pecuniary reward has come from what is called serial publication in this or that magazine or newspaper

as from book publication. Apart from fiction,
access to magazines and newspapers has become,
if it has not always been, an easy and pleasant way
of making oneself heard upon the subject nearest
to one's heart. Literary journalists, who have
afterwards republished their contributions in
volume form include Sydney Smith and John
Wilson at the beginning of the reign; as
also Douglas Jerrold, Mark Lemon, Edmund
Yates, Charles Mackay, and George Augustus
Sala. **Sydney Smith** left nothing that we can 1771-1845
read to-day. He lives as a pleasant memory. We
know that he must have been a liberal-minded, as
he was certainly a very witty clergyman. He wrote
on " The Ballot " in 1837 and on " The Church
Bills " in 1838, and he went on writing zealously
until his death. " The Wit and Wisdom of Sydney
Smith " was published in 1861. **John Wilson** has 1785-1854
a more purely literary record. As editor of *Blackwood's Magazine*, he made that publication a power
in the land. His " Recreations of Christopher
North " appeared in 1842. Many of his essays
and sketches may still be read with real pleasure,
and indeed his influence will be very much alive
for many a year to come. **Douglas Jerrold** is also 1803-1857
well known to-day by his " Black-eyed Susan "
and " Mrs Caudle's Curtain Lectures." His son,
Blanchard Jerrold (1826-1884), wrote his life.
Mark Lemon was one of the first editors of *Punch* 1809-1870

newspaper. His hundreds of articles and many novels are all well nigh forgotten, but his name will always receive honourable mention in the history 1831-1894 of journalism. **Edmund Yates,** who founded *The World* newspaper in 1874, will be remembered by his well written "Autobiography"—one of the best books of the kind ever issued. Yates wrote many novels, but they have all passed out of 1814-1889 memory. **Charles Mackay** was an active journalist for a number of years. He wrote novels, poems, and criticisms, and an entertaining autobiography entitled "Forty Years' Recollections of Life, Literature, and Public Affairs." Dr Mackay was father of Eric Mackay, author of "Love Letters of a Violinist," and stepfather of Miss Marie Corelli 1828-1895 the novelist. **George Augustus Sala,** who wrote so continuously for the *Daily Telegraph* and other journals, was also author of many books as well as the inevitable autobiography. "The Land of the Golden Fleece," "America Revisited," and "Living London" are well known. **Richard** 1848-1887 **Jefferies** published his "Gamekeeper at Home" in the *Pall Mall Gazette.* "Wood Magic" (1881), "Bevis" (1882), and "The Story of My Heart" (1883), are his best books.

These names suggest a hundred others. The most honoured journalist of to-day is **Frederick** 1830- **Greenwood,** who has edited "The Cornhill

Magazine" and more than one newspaper. He has written poems, stories, and essays, his "Lover's Lexicon" and "Dreams" being two of his latest volumes.

Another editor of *The Cornhill Magazine*, **James Payn**, has written many successful novels, of which "Lost Sir Massingberd" (1864) and "By Proxy" (1878) are perhaps the most popular. Mr Payn's many accomplishments, his delightful humour and gift of genial anecdote, have endeared him to a wide circle. **1830-**

A journalist of equal distinction was **Richard Holt Hutton**, the editor of the *Spectator*, who in that journal maintained for thirty-five years the high-water mark of dignified and independent criticism, in an age in which the extensive intercourse of authors and critics, the constant communication between the writers of books and the writers for newspapers, has made independent criticism a difficult, and, indeed, almost impossible achievement. Mr Hutton wrote many books, two of the most notable being "Essays Literary and Speculative," which were full of thoughtful and discerning estimates of the works of Wordsworth, George Eliot, and other writers. **1826-1897**

Memoirs abound in the epoch, although we are mainly indebted to translations. Amiel's "Journal," translated by Mrs Humphry Ward,

"Marie Bashkirtseff's Diary," translated by Mathilde Blind, reflect one side of this literary taste; while the thousand and one memoirs concerning Napoleon I. represents another. The most popular series of political memoirs in English we owed to **Charles Cavendish Fulke** 1794-1865 **Greville,** who became Clerk to the Privy Council in 1821, and held that post until 1860. After his death his diary was edited by Mr Henry Reeve. The first series of the "Greville Memoirs" dealing with the reign of George IV. and William IV., appeared in 1875 and created immense excitement.[1] The later volumes excited less interest.

"The Life of the late Prince Consort" (1874) by 1816- **Sir Theodore Martin,** naturally contained no indiscretions although it did much to enhance, if that were possible, kindly memories of the Queen's husband. Sir Theodore Martin made

[1] A contemporary epigram thus expressed the general feeling :

"For fifty years he listened at the door,
And heard some scandal, but invented more.
This he wrote down ; and statesmen, queens, and kings,
Appear before us quite as common things.
Most now are dead ; yet some few still remain
To whom these ' Memoirs ' give a needless pain ;
For though they laugh, and say ' 'Tis only Greville,'
They wish him and his ' Memoirs ' at the D—l."

his first fame under the pseudonym of Bon
Gaultier. His "Book of Ballads," written in con-
junction with Professor Aytoun, had much suc-
cess. Sir Theodore Martin also wrote Aytoun's
"Memoir" (1867), and "The Life of Lord
Lyndhurst" (1883). He has translated the Odes
of Horace, "The Vita Nuova" of Dante, Goethe's
"Faust," and Heine's "Poems and Ballads." In
1885 he published a "Sketch of the Life of
Princess Alice."

It is difficult to know where to place **Sir Arthur 1817-1875
Helps,** who wrote plays, novels, histories, and
essays. He was an overrated writer in his time.
He is perhaps underrated now. Two series of
"Friends in Council" appeared, the first in 1847,
the second in 1859. They dealt with all manner
of abstract subjects, such as "war," "despotism,"
and so on, and were very popular. Another
volume, "Companions of my Solitude," was
equally successful. Helps was rash enough to
enter into competition with Prescott in treating
of the Spanish Conquest of America; but the
picturesque books of the earlier writer are still
with us while Helps's "Life of Pizarro" (1869)
and "Life of Cortes" (1871) are almost forgotten.
That also is the fate of his romance, "Realmah"
(1868) and of his tragedies, "Catherine Douglas"
and "Henry II." Sir Arthur Helps was Clerk to

the Privy Council, and he edited the "Principal Speeches and Addresses of the late Prince Consort" (1862).

Sir Arthur Helps also edited for **Queen Victoria** her "Leaves from a Journal of our Life in the Highlands" (1868). The Queen has also published "The Early Days of His Royal Highness the Prince Consort" (1867), and "More Leaves from the Journal of our Life in the Highlands" (1884).

Her Majesty has been credited with a genuine taste for letters, and a love for good poetry and good fiction. With some show of authority it has been stated that her favourite novelists are Sir Walter Scott, Miss Austen, and Miss Brontë; while it is quite evident to the least inquisitive that many literary theologians have had some measure of her regard. Happily the times have long passed when literature needed the patronage of the powerful. To-day it can honourably stand alone. But it is pleasing to remember that the sovereign whose sixty years of rule make so remarkable a record in literature, as in many other aspects of the world's progress, has taken a sympathetic interest in the books and bookmen of the epoch.

The Queen will have seen reputations blaze forth and flicker out ignominiously; she will have seen many a writer hailed for immortal to-day and forgotten to-morrow. She will have seen, however, a succession of writers, Browning and Tennyson, Carlyle and Ruskin, most notable of all, who in their impulse towards high ideals of human brotherhood, in their enthusiasm of humanity, have given us a literature without a parallel in history; and she will not be without a sense of gratification that that literature will go down the ages bearing the name of Victorian.

INDEX

ABBOTT, Edwin. Distinguished member of Broad Church party; 'Philochristus' and 'Onesimus'; his 'Through Nature to Christ' perhaps the best evidence of the development of his party, 165.

Abbott, Evelyn, 163.

'Adam Bede,' 49; Reade on, 50.

'Addresses and Reviews,' 158.

'Admiral's Daughter, The,' 71.

'Adventures of Harry Richmond, The,' 61.

'Agnes Grey,' 47, 48.

'Agriculture and Prices, History of,' 144.

'A Hard Struggle,' 38.

Ainsworth, W. H. 'Old St Paul's,' 'The Tower of London,' and 'Rookwood' his best novels, 67.

'Alec Forbes of Howglen,' 63.

Alexander, Mrs (Mrs Hector), 74.

'Alexander the Great,' 33.

'Alice's Adventures in Wonderland,' 64.

Allen, Grant. 'Anglo-Saxon Britain,' 99.

'All in All,' 39.

'All Sorts and Conditions of Men,' 65.

Allingham, William. Writer of Celtic and Irish poems and ballads; edited *Fraser's Magazine*, 173.

All the Year Round, 69.

A. L. O. E. (Miss Charlotte Maria Tucker). Most popular stories, 'Pride and his Pursuers,' 'Exiles in Babylon,' 'House Beautiful,' and 'Cyril Ashley,' 73.

'Alton Locke,' 53.

'America Revisited,' 188.

'Amiel's Journal,' 189.

'And Shall Trelawney Die,' 38.

'Angel in the House, The,' 31.

'Anglo-Saxon Britain,' 99.

'Animal Intelligence,' 157.

'Ann Sherwood,' 72.

'Annals of the Parish,' 63.

'Anthony Hope,' 63.

'Anthropology' (Tylor's), 99.

'Antiquity of Man, The,' 153.

Anti-theological books. The three most notable, 170.

'Apologia pro Vitâ Suâ,' 110.

'Appreciations,' 171.

Archer, William, 175.

Aristotle's 'Politics,' Jowett's translation, 163.

Arnold, Dr. 'History of Rome,' 102. (*Vide infra.*)

Arnold, Matthew, and Wordsworth, 8; his poetic gifts first recognised by Swinburne, 17; 'Literature and Dogma'; 'God and the Bible'; influence on contemporary religious thought, 18; Professor of Poetry; 'Essays in Criticism'; definition of criticism;

Index

educational work, 19; best known by his poetry, 19, 20, 171; 'Empedocles on Etna'; 'The Strayed Reveller'; 'Poems,' 20; 'Thyrsis,' 21; admiration for Emily Brontë, 47.

Arnold, Sir Edwin. 'Light of Asia' and 'Light of the World,' 26; on Henry Kingsley, 56.

Arnold, Thomas. At Rugby; Dr Hawkins' recommendation; his methods; 'Thucydides'; 'History of Rome'; a purifying influence, 160; at first unpopular; reaction in his favour; his best known pupils, 161. (*Vide supra.*)

Ashley, Professor W. J. 'Economic History and Theory,' 144.

Athenæum, The, and Tupper's 'Proverbial Philosophy,' 27.

Aunt Judy's Magazine, 73.

'Aurora Leigh,' 14.

Austin, Alfred. Laureate, 39; 'The Golden Age'; 'Savonarola'; 'English Lyrics,' etc., 40.

'Autobiography of W. B. Scott,' 173.

'Autobiography' (Mill), 138, 142.

'Autobiography' (Yates), 188.

'Ave atque Vale,' 17.

'Ayrshire Legatees,' 63.

Aytoun, Professor, 191.

BAGEHOT, Walter. A great authority on banking and finance; 'Physics and Politics'; 'Economic Studies'; 'Literary Studies,' 184.

Bailey, Philip James; author of 'Festus,' 28.

Bain, Alexander. Assisted Mill in his 'Logic'; 'The Senses and the Intellect'; 'The Emotions and the Will'; 'Mental and Moral Science'; style, 147.

Balfour, Francis Maitland, 151.

'Ballades in Blue China,' 30, 176.

'Ballads and Lyrics of Old France,' 176.

'Ballads for the Times,' 27.

'Ballot, The,' 187.

Banim, John and Michael, 34.

'Barchester Towers,' 58.

Barham, Richard Harris. 'Ingoldsby Legends' first appeared in *Bentley's Miscellany*; his novel, 'My Cousin Nicholas,' all but forgotten, 30.

'Barnaby Rudge,' 42.

Barnes, William. Philologist and poet; author of 'Poems of Rural Life in the Dorset Dialect,' 37.

'Barrack-Room Ballads,' 40.

Barrie, J. M. 'A Window in Thrums,' written before he had read Dr MacDonald's books; probably influenced by John Galt, 63.

'Barry Cornwall,' 35-36.

Beagle, The, 154.

'Beau Austin,' 60.

'Beauchamp's Career,' 61.

Beddoes, Thomas Lovell, author of 'The Bride's Tragedy' and 'Death's Jest Book,' 36.

Bell, Currer, Ellis, and Acton, 47, 48.

Bentham, Jeremy, 137.

Bentinck, Lord George. Biography of, by Lord Beaconsfield, 57.

Bentley, Robert, 151.

Bentley's Miscellany and 'Ingoldsby Legends,' 30.

Besant, Sir Walter. 'All Sorts and Conditions of Men,' practical

Index

influence of; collaboration with James Rice; 'Ready Money Mortiboy'; 'The Golden Butterfly,' 65.

'Bevis,' 188.

'Bible Inspiration,' 168.

'Biographical History of Philosophy,' 148-149.

'Biographical Sketches,' 180.

'Black but Comely,' 59.

Black, William. First appearance as a novelist in 'Love or Marriage,' 68; 'A Daughter of Heth'; 'Madcap Violet'; 'Macleod of Dare,' 69.

'Black-eyed Susan,' 187.

Blackmore, Richard Doddridge. 'Lorna Doone,' received coldly at first; an unexcelled master of rustic comedy; 'The Maid of Sker'; 'Christowell'; 'Cripps, the Carrier,' 69.

Blackwood's Magazine, 49, 70, 74, 187.

'Blessed Damozel, The,' 23.

Blind, Mathilde. Translated 'Marie Bashkirtseff's Diary,' 190.

'Blot in the 'Scutcheon, A,' 12.

'Book of Ballads' (Martin and Aytoun), 191.

'Book of Verses,' 172.

Boole. The Logician, 147.

Booth, Charles. 'Life and Labor of the People,' 144-145.

'Borderers, The,' 9.

Borrow, George. The most famous traveller of the reign; 'Bible in Spain'; 'Lavengro'; 'The Romany Rye,' 185.

'Botanic Garden, The,' 154.

Braddon, Miss, 74.

Bradley, Professor A. C. Editor

of Green's 'Prolegomena,' and author of 'Ethical Studies,' 148.

Brewer, Rev. John Sherren. Chief work a 'Calendar of Letters and Papers of the Reign of Henry VIII.,' 88; 'The Reign of Henry VIII.,' 89.

Brewster, Sir David. The first writer of the era to popularise science; founder of *Edinburgh Cyclopædia*; his 'Life of Newton,' 'Martyrs of Science,' and 'More Worlds than One' still widely read, 150.

'Bride's Tragedy, The,' 36.

Bridgewater Treatises, 153.

Bright, James Franck. 'English History for the use of Public Schools,' 97.

'British Novelists and their Styles,' 177.

Broad Church party, manifesto of, 162.

Brontë, Anne. 'Poems'; 'Agnes Grey,' 47; 'The Tenant of Wildfell Hall,' 48.

Brontë, Charlotte. Early years, 46; Brussels; 'Poems'; 'The Professor'; 'Jane Eyre'; 'Shirley'; 'Villette'; marriage and death, 47½; Mrs Gaskell's 'Life,' 71.

Brontë, Emily. 'Poems'; 'Wuthering Heights'; 'Last Lines'; 'The Old Stoic,' 47; Swinburne's criticism of 'Wuthering Heights,' 48.

Brooke, Stopford Augustus. Secession from the Church of England; 'Primer of English Literature,' 'History of Early English Poetry,' 'Theology in

Index

the English Poets,' and 'Life of Milton,' 166.

Broughton, Miss Rhoda, 74.

Browne, Hablot, 45.

Browning, Elizabeth Barrett, 13; not in the least incomprehensible; 'Cry of the Children'; 'Cowper's Grave'; 'Aurora Leigh'; 'Sonnets from the Portuguese'; her opinion of 'Aurora Leigh'; 'Casa Guidi Windows'; death, 14.

Browning, Robert. Friendship with Tennyson; social traits, 11; superb characterisation; charge of obscurity; half his work not obscure; 'The Ring and the Book'; 'Men and Women'; and 'Dramatic Idyls' are exciting stories; 'Luria'; 'In a Balcony'; and 'A Blot in the 'Scutcheon' as readable as railway novels; his small audience, 12; 'Pauline'; hard fight for recognition; Elizabeth Barrett's appreciation; marriage, 13-14.

Bryce, James. 'The Holy Roman Empire'; parliamentary life, 104.

Buckland, Frank. Author of books on 'Natural History,' 153.

Buckland, William. Author of 'Geology and Mineralogy considered with reference to Natural Theology,' 153.

Buckle, Henry Thomas. 'History of Civilization in England'; defects of, 103.

Burney, Fanny, 49.

Burton, John Hill. 'History of Scotland,' 96.

'By Proxy,' 189.

Byron, death of, 5; attitude towards Wordsworth, 8.

CAIRD, Edward. 'Philosophy of Kant'; 'Essays on Literature and Philosophy'; 'The Evolution of Religion,' 170.

Cairnes, John Elliott, 143.

'Calendar of Letters and Papers of the Reign of Henry VIII., A,' 88.

'Calendar of Spanish State Papers of Elizabeth,' 89.

'Called to be Saints,' 22.

'Callista,' 111.

Calverley, Charles Stuart. One of the most famous successors of Hood and Barham; wrote 'Fly Leaves' and 'Verses and Translations,' 30.

Campbell, James Dykes. Biographer of Coleridge, 178.

Campbell, Lewis, 163.

Carleton, William. 'Traits and Stories of the Irish Peasantry'; 'Tales of Ireland'; 'Fardorougha the Miser'; 'Black Prophet,' 66.

Carlyle, Thomas. Birth; education; his father's influence, 112; as tutor; biographer; Madame de Staël's influence, 113; veneration for Goethe, 113-114, 120-121; 'Wilhelm Meister'; 'Life of Schiller,' 113; marriage; Richter's influence, 114; personal character, 115-120; domestic relations, 115-120; Froude's 'Letters' and Reminiscences, 115-116; his influence, 118-119, 128; intentions respecting 'Reminiscences,' 119-120; 'Sartor Resartus'; *Fraser's Magazine*, 121; influence of his teaching on younger minds,

Index

199

Index

Index

Index

Index

Index

Life'; 'Adam Bede,' 49; 'The Mill on the Floss'; 'Silas Marner'; 'Romola'; 'Felix Holt'; 'Middlemarch'; 'Daniel Deronda'; marriage; death; her letters a disappointment; her poetry; 'Spanish Gipsy'; 'Choir Invisible'; 'by her novels she must be judged,' 50; catholicity of sympathy, 51-52; has not maintained her position, but has an assured place, 53.

Eliot, George, and Spencer, 145.

Eliza Cook's Journal, 29.

Elliott, Ebenezer. Author of 'Corn Law Rhymes,' &c., 37.

'Emotions and the Will, The,' 147.

'Empedocles on Etna,' 20.

'Endeavour after the Christian Life,' 167.

'English History and Commerce, Growth of,' 144.

'English History for the Use of Public Schools,' 97.

'English in Ireland, The,' 88.

'English Lyrics,' 40.

'English Men of Letters Series,' 181.

'English Seamen in the Sixteenth Century,' 88.

'Englishwomen of Letters,' 72.

'Enigmas of Life,' 170.

'Eothen,' 96.

'Epic of Hades,' 26.

'Epic of Women and other Poems,' 39.

'Esmond,' 45.

'Essay in Aid of the Grammar of Assent,' 111.

'Essay on Ritualism,' 106.

'Essays and Reviews,' 162.

'Essays and Studies,' 17.

'Essays,' by T. E. C. Leslie, 144.

'Essays, Classical and Modern' (Myers), 172.

'Essays in Criticism' (Arnold), 19.

'Essays, Literary and Speculative' (Hutton), 189.

'Essays on Literature and Philosophy' (Caird), 170.

'Essays on Unsettled Questions in Political Economy' (Mill), 140.

'Ethical Studies,' 148.

'Ethical Theory, Types of,' 167.

'Euclid and his Modern Rivals,' 64.

'European Morals from Augustus to Charlemagne,' 96.

'Evan Harrington,' 61.

Evans, Mary Ann (George Eliot), 49-53.

'Evolution of Religion, The,' 170.

Ewing, Mrs. Author of 'Remembrances of Mrs Overtheway,' 73.

'Examination of Sir William Hamilton's Philosophy,' 140.

'Excursion, The,' 9.

'Exiles in Babylon,' 73.

'Expansion of England, The,' 105.

'FACE OF THE DEEP, The,' 22.

Faraday, Michael. Famous physicist; Royal Institution Lectures; 'Magneto-electricity'; devotion to science, 150.

'Faraday as a Discoverer,' 150.

'Fardorougha the Miser,' 66.

'Far from the Madding Crowd,' 68.

'Farina,' 61.

Farrar, Frederick William, 168.

'Faust' (Martin's translation), 191.

Fawcett, Henry. A disciple of the Ricardo school; 'Manual of

204

Index

Political Economy,' 142-143; a critic of Indian finance; Postmaster-General, 143.

Ferguson, Sir Samuel, 34.

'Felix Holt,' 50.

Ferrier, James Frederick. Professor of moral philosophy at St Andrews; 'Lectures in Greek Philosophy,' 169.

'Festus,' 27, 28.

Finlay, George. 'A History of Greece from its Conquest by the Romans to the Present Time'; Greek War of Independence, 102.

'First Principles' (Spencer's), 145.

Fitzgerald, Edward. 'Letters and Literary Remains' and 'Omar Khayyám,' 35.

'Fly-Leaves,' 30.

'Footprints of Former Men in Far Cornwall,' 38.

'Footprints of the Creator,' 152.

'Fors Clavigera,' 133-134.

Forster, John. 'Life of Swift'; 'Life of Walter Savage Landor'; 'Goldsmith'; 'Dickens'; 'Life of Sir John Eliot,' 178; 'Statesmen of the Commonwealth,' 179.

Fortnightly Review, 93, 181.

'Forty Years' Recollections of Life, Literature and Public Affairs,' 188.

Foster, Michael, 151.

'Foul Play,' 58.

Fox, Charles James, and 'Madoc,' 6; 'Early History of,' 182.

'Framley Parsonage,' 58.

'Frank Mildmay,' 67.

Fraser's Magazine, 45, 173.

'Frederick II. of Prussia,' 124, 126, 127.

Freeman, Edward A. First work, 'A History of Architecture';

'History of Federal Government'; 'History of the Norman Conquest'; 'Reign of William Rufus'; 'Old English History,' 81; not a metaphysician; the 'Norman Conquest,' worth the effort of reading it; Regius Professor at Oxford, 82; contrasted with Froude, 83.

'French Revolution,' 124, 125.

'Frenchwomen of Letters,' 72.

'Friends in Council,' 191.

Froude, James Anthony. Contrasted with Freeman; abandoned supernatural Christianity, 83; 'The Spirit's Trials'; 'The Lieutenant's Daughter'; 'Nemesis of Faith'; his great work, 'The History of England,' 84; his style and sympathies, 85; the 'À Becket' articles inaccurate; his 'Life of Carlyle'; Sir Fitz James Stephen's defence of the 'Life,' 86-87; 'Short Studies on Great Subjects'; 'Life of Bunyan'; 'Life of Cæsar'; Carlyle's influence in 'The English in Ireland'; 'Lectures on the Council of Trent'; 'English Seamen in the Sixteenth Century'; 'Life and Letters of Erasmus,' 88.

Froude, Richard Hurrell. 'Literary Remains of,' 83.

Fullerton, Lady Georgina. Author of 'Ann Sherwood,' 72.

GAIRDNER, James. 'Life and Reign of Richard III.,' 96.

'Gamekeeper at Home, The,' 188.

Gardiner, Samuel Rawson. The Historian of the Stuart kings; now well into the study of the

Index

Protectorate, 89; minor works, 'The Gunpowder Plot'; 'Cromwell's Place in History'; not a brilliant writer, but absolutely fair and impartial; his books the safest guide to the period, 90.

Garnett, Richard (Doctor), and Marston, 38; a partisan of Shelley; an acute critic, 174.

Gaskell, Mrs. 'Mary Barton' her first success; 'Ruth,' 'North and South,' 'Sylvia's Lovers,' 'Cranford,' and 'The Life of Charlotte Brontë' her most enduring works, 71.

Gatty, Mrs, 73.

'Gebir,' 15.

Geikie, James. 'The Great Ice Age,' 153.

Geikie, Sir Archibald. His 'Text Book of Geology' a model of lucid writing, 153.

'Geoffrey Hamlyn,' 55.

'Geology and Mineralogy considered with reference to Natural Theology,' 153.

'Geology, Principles of' (Lyell's), 152.

'Geology, Text Book of' (Geikie's) 153.

Germ, The, 23.

Gibbon's 'Rome,' Milman's edition of, 102.

'Glaciers, On the Structure and Motion of,' 151.

'Gladiators, The,' 59.

Gladstone, William Ewart, and Macaulay, 93; 'The State in its Relations with the Church'; Macaulay's review; 'Essay on Ritualism'; and 'The Vatican Decrees'; 'Studies in Homer';

'Gleanings'; on Newman's secession, 106.

'Gleanings' (W. E. Gladstone), 106.

'Goblin Market,' 22.

'God and the Bible,' 18.

'Golden Age, The,' 40.

'Golden Butterfly, The,' 65.

'Golden Treasury of Songs and Lyrics, The,' 81.

Goldsmith, 41; Life of, 178.

Gosse, Edmund. A poet and critic; joint translator with Mr Wm. Archer of *Ibsen*, 175; best biography, 'Life of Gray,' 175.

'Government, A Dialogue on the best form of,' 184.

'Government, On the Proper Sphere of,' 145.

'Grammar of Assent,' 111.

'Great Ice Age, The,' 153.

'Greece, History of' (Cox's), 100.

'Greece, History of' (Finlay's), 102.

'Greece, History of' (Grote's), 100, 101.

Greece, History of' (Thirlwall's), 101.

Green, Alice Stopford. 'Town Life in the Fifteenth Century,' 98.

Green, John Richard. 'Short History of the English People'; place as a historian, 97; critics, 97-98; enlarged edition; dedication; Bishop Stubbs and Professor Freeman; 'The Making of England,'; 'The Conquest of England'; Sir Archibald Geikie's tribute; adverse criticisms, 98.

Green, Thomas Hill. Long a leader of the Hegelian philosophy at Oxford; published through *Contemporary Review*

Index

articles on ' Mr Herbert Spencer and Mr G. H. Lewes: their Application of the Doctrine of Evolution to Thought,' 147 ; his ' Prolegomena to Ethics,' finally edited by Professor Bradley ; a moral force in Oxford apart from his philosophy, 148.

Greenwood, Frederick. The most honoured journalist of to-day ; edited *Cornhill Magazine*, 188 ; writer of poems, stories, and essays ; ' Lover's Lexicon ' ; ' Dreams,' 189.

Greg, William Rathbone. Antitheological writer ; ' The Creed of Christendom ' ; ' Enigmas of Life ' ; ' Rocks Ahead,' 170.

Greville, Charles Cavendish Fulke. His political memoirs the most popular series we have, 190.

' Greville Memoirs,' 190.

' Griffith Gaunt,' 58.

Grote, George. *Westminster Review*, 100 ; M.P. for the City of London ; ' History of Greece ' ; Bishop Thirlwall's appreciation, 101 ; influence respecting views of Athenian democracy, 102.

Grote and J. S. Mill, 139.

' Growth of English History and Commerce,' 144.

' Gryll Grange,' 63.

' Gunpowder Plot, The,' 90.

HALLAM, Henry. ' View of the State of Europe during the Middle Ages,' 77 ; ' Constitutional History of England' ; ' Introduction to the Literature of Europe in the Fifteenth, Sixteenth, and Seventeenth Centuries,' 78.

Hamerton, Philip Gilbert. Author of ' Marmorne,' 171 ; intimately acquainted with French life ; edited *The Portfolio ;* ' The Intellectual Life,' 172.

' Hand and Soul,' 23.

' Handy Andy,' 34.

' Hard Cash,' 58.

Hardy, Thomas. Earlier fame won with ' Far from the Madding Crowd ' ; later popularity by Tess of the D'Urbervilles,' ' The Return of the Native,' and ' The Woodlanders ' greater than either, 68.

' Harold,' 10, 56.

Harrison, Frederic. A gifted Positivist ; ' Order and Progress ' ; ' Choice of Books,' 179.

' Harry Lorrequer,' 66.

Hawker, Robert Stephen. Author of ' Song of the Western Men,' and ' Footprints of Former Men in Far Cornwall,' 38.

' Headlong Hall,' 62.

Heine's ' Poems and Ballads ' (Martin's translation), 191.

Helps, Sir Arthur. ' Friends in Council ' ; ' Companions of my Solitude ' ; ' Life of Pizarro ' ; ' Life of Cortes ' ; ' Realmah ' ; ' Catherine Douglas ' ; ' Henry II ,' 191 ; edited ' Principal Speeches and Addresses of the late Prince Consort,' and ' Leaves from a Journal,' 192.

Henley, William Ernest. ' Book of Verses ' ; ' Song of the Sword ' ; a critic of exceptional vigour ; ' Views and Reviews,' 172.

Henley, W. E., and Stevenson, 60.

Hennell, Sarah, 49.

Index

Index

'History of England, 1830-1873' (Molesworth), 95.

'History of English Poetry' (Courthope), 178.

'History of English Thought in the Eighteenth Century' (Stephen), 175.

'History of France previous to the Revolution' (Kitchin), 103.

'History of Federal Government' (Freeman), 81.

'History of Greece' (Cox), 100.

'History of Greece' (Finlay), 102.

'History of Greece' (Grote), 100-102.

'History of Greece' (Thirlwall), 101.

'History of Normandy and England' (Palgrave), 81.

'History of Our Own Time, 1830-1897 (MacCarthy), 95.

'History of Rome' (Arnold), 102, 160.

'History of Samuel Titmarsh and the Great Hoggarty Diamond, The,' 45.

'History of Scotland' (Burton), 96.

'History of Trade Unionism, The' (Webb), 145.

'History of the Church of England' (Molesworth), 95.

'History of the Eighteenth Century' (Lecky), 96.

'History of the Four Georges' (MacCarthy), 96.

'History of the Jews' (Milman), 102.

'History of the Norman Conquest' (Freeman), 81.

'History of the Papacy from the Great Schism to the Sack of Rome' (Creighton), 103.

'History of the Peace' (Martineau), 95.

'History of the Romans under the Empire (Merivale), 102.

'History of the Reign of Queen Anne' (Stanhope), 95.

'History of the War in the Crimea,' (Kinglake), 96.

'Holy Roman Empire, The,' 104.

'Homer' (Lang's translation), 176.

'Homer, Studies in,' 106.

Hood, Thomas. 'Song of the Shirt' and 'Dream of Eugene Aram' most popular, 29.

Hooker, Sir Joseph, 151.

Horne, Richard Hengist. Wrote 'Orion,' 'Judas Iscariot,' 'The Death of Marlowe,' &c., 36.

Houghton, Lord (Monckton Milnes). 'Life, Letters, and Literary Remains of John Keats'; his life written by Sir Wemyss Reid, 183.

'Hour and the Man, The,' 181.

'Hours in a Library, 175.

'Hours of Thought on Sacred Things,' 167.

'House Beautiful,' 73.

'House of Life, The,' 24.

Howson, John Saul. Joint authorship with Rev. W. J. Conybeare of 'The Life and Epistles of St Paul,' 168.

Hughes, Thomas. A pupil of Dr Arnold's; wrote finest boy's book in the language, 'Tom Brown's School Days,' 161.

Hume, Major Martin. 'The Year after the Armada'; 'The Courtships of Queen Elizabeth'; 'Calendar of Spanish State Papers of Elizabeth,' 89.

Index

Index

Index

Index

Index

ham'; 'Zanoni'; 'Harold';
'Rienzi'; 'The Last of the
Barons'; 'The Last Days of
Pompeii'; 'The Caxtons';
'Money'; 'Richelieu'; 'The
Lady of Lyons'; one of the
'cleverest' men of his age, 56.

MACAULAY, Thomas Babington.
His work guided by rhetorical
principles; earliest efforts in
Quarterly Magazine and *Edinburgh Review*; Jeffrey on his
'Milton,' 91; qualities of his
'Essays'; his career; 'History
of England from the Accession of
James II.' very successful, 92;
now severely criticised, 93; in
spite of its deficiencies, a great
work, 94-95.

Macaulay and Hawker, 38.

MacCarthy, Justin. 'History of
Our Own Time, 1830-1897,' 95;
'History of the Four Georges,'96.

MacDonald, George. 'Robert
Falconer'; 'David Elginbrod';
'Alec Forbes of Howglen,' 63.

Mackay, Charles. Novelist, poet
and critic; 'Forty Years' Recollections of Life, Literature and
Public Affairs,' 188.

Mackay, Eric. 'Love Letters of
a Violinist,' 188.

'Macleod of Dare,' 69.

Macquoid, Mrs, 74.

Macmillan's Magazine, 181.

'Madcap Violet,' 69.

'Madeleine,' 72.

'Madoc,' 6.

Mahon, Lord, 95.

'Maiden and Married Life of Mary
Powell,' 72.

'Maid of Sker, The,' 69.

'Maid Marion,' 62.

'Makers of Florence,' 74.

'Making of England, The,' 98.

Malet, Lucas, 74.

Manchester Examiner and Ruskin,
133.

Mangan, James Clarence, 34.

Manning, Anne. Author of
'Maiden and Married Life of
Mary Powell,' 72.

Manning, Cardinal. Books and
sermons of theological interest
only; his 'Life,' 169.

Mansel, Henry Longueville. 'The
Limits of Religious Thought';
'Metaphysics, or the Philosophy
of Consciousness, Phenomenal
and Real'; a skilful fighter,
169.

'Manual of Political Economy'
(Fawcett's), 142.

'Marie Bashkirtseff's Diary,' 190.

'Marcian Colonna,' 36.

'Marie de Méranie,' 38.

'Marius the Epicurean,' 171.

'Marmorne,' 171.

Marryat, Captain Frederick.
'Frank Mildmay'; 'Mr Midshipman Easy'; 'Peter Simple';
editor of *Metropolitan Magazine;*
appreciated by Carlyle and
Ruskin, 66-67.

Marsh, Mrs. Author of 'The
Admiral's Daughter' and 'The
Deformed,' 71.

Marshall, Alfred. Author of
'Economics of Industry' and
'Principles of Economics,' 143.

Marston, John Westland. Author
of 'Strathmore,' 'Marie de
Méranie,' and 'A Hard
Struggle,' 38.

Marston, Philip Bourke. Pub-

Index

lished 'Song Tide and other Poems,' 'All in All,' and 'Wind Voices,' 39.

Martin, Sir Theodore. 'Life of the late Prince Consort,' 190; 'Book of Ballads'; 'Memoir of Aytoun'; 'Life of Lord Lyndhurst'; translated the Odes of Horace; 'The Vita Nuova'; 'Faust'; and Heine's 'Poems and Ballads'; 'Sketch of the Life of Princess Alice,' 191.

Martineau, Harriet. 'History of the Peace,' 95; Abridgment of Comte; influence upon her own generation; very versatile writer; her 'Biographical Sketches' originally published in *Daily News*, 180; her historical work mere compilation; 'Deerbrook'; 'The Hour and the Man'; 'Letters on the Laws of Man's Nature and Development,' 181.

Martineau, James. Early career, 166; from Bentham to Kant; 'Endeavour after the Christian Life'; 'Hours of Thought on Sacred Things'; 'Study of Spinoza'; 'Types of Ethical Theory,' 167.

'Martyrs of Science,' 150.

'Mary Barton,' 71.

'Mary Tudor,' 33.

'Masks and Faces,' 58.

Massey, Gerald. Chartist poet. Wrote 'Poems and Charms' and 'Voices of Freedom and Lyrics of Love,' &c., 37.

Massey, William Nathaniel. 'History of England under George III.,' 95.

Masson, David. 'Life of Milton';

'British Novelists and their Styles'; 'Drummond of Hawthornden,' 177.

'Master of Ballantrae, The,' 60.

'Maud,' 10.

'Maude,' 22.

Maurice, John Frederick Denison. Editor of the *Athenæum;* joined the Anglican Church, 163; 'Subscription no Bondage'; 'Kingdom of Christ' tracts; 'Politics for the People'; organised the Christian socialist and co-operative movement, 164.

Maxse, Admiral, 62.

May, Sir Thomas Erskine. Continued the work of Hallam and Stubbs, 79; 'Democracy in Europe'; 'Constitutional History,' 80.

Melbourne, Lord, and Macaulay, 91.

'Melincourt,' 62.

Melville, George John Whyte. The novelist of the hunting field; 'Katerfelto'; 'Black but Comely'; 'The Queen's Maries'; 'The Gladiators,' 59.

'Memoirs of Barry Lyndon,' 45.

'Memoir of Principal Tulloch,' 74.

'Memorials of Canterbury,' 161.

'Men and Women,' 12.

'Mental and Moral Science,' 147.

'Mental Evolution in Animals,' 157.

Meredith, George. 'Love in a Valley,' 60; The Browning of Novelists; 'The Shaving of Shagpat'; 'Farina'; 'The Ordeal of Richard Feverel' considered his best novel; 'Evan Harrington'; 'Rhoda Fleming'; 'The Adventures of Harry Richmond';

Index

'Beauchamp's Career'; 'The Egoist'; 'The Tragic Comedians'; 'Diana of the Crossways'; Stevenson's admiration for 'The Egoist,' 61 ; 'Sandra Belloni,' 62.

Meredith, George, and Rossetti, 24.

Merivale, Charles. 'History of the Romans under the Empire,' 102.

'Metaphysics, or the Philosophy of Consciousness, Phenomenal and Real,' 169.

Methodism and Carlyle, 51.

'Methods of Ethics,' 143.

Metropolitan Magazine, The, 67.

'Middle Ages' (Hallam's), 77.

'Middlemarch,' 50.

Mill, James. 'History of India'; 'Analysis of the Human Mind,' 137.

Mill, John Stuart. Ruskin's scorn of; education, 137 ; influence of Wordsworth ; the India House ; *Westminster Review* ; Carlyle's 'French Revolution,' 138 ; 'Political Economy'; 'Liberty'; 'Subjection of Women'; contemporary opinion of Mrs Mill, 139 ; 'Logic'; 'Essays on Unsettled Questions in Political Economy'; 'Principles of Political Economy'; 'Liberty'; 'Sir William Hamilton's Philosophy'; 'Dissertations and Discussions'; 'Considerations on Representative Government'; a stimulator of public opinion, 140 ; his philosophical weaknesses, 141-42 ; abandonment of early positions ; 'Autobiography'; a socialist at the last, 142.

Miller, Hugh, 151. Journalist ; *The Witness;* 'Old Red Sandstone'; 'Footprints of the Creator'; 'The Testimony of the Rocks,' 152.

'Mill on the Floss, The,' 50.

Millais, Sir John, and the pre-Raphaelite movement, 23.

Milman, Henry Hart. 'Gibbon's Rome'; 'History of the Jews'; 'History of Christianity under the Empire,' 102 ; 'Latin Christianity'; Dean Stanley's appreciation, 103.

'Milton, Masson's Life of,' 177.

'Ministering Children,' 73.

Minor Poet, The, of our era, 31.

'Mirandola,' 36.

'Mr Herbert Spencer and Mr G. H. Lewes ; their application of the Doctrine of Evolution to Thought,' 147.

'Mr Midshipman Easy,' 67.

'Mrs Caudle's Curtain Lectures,' 187.

'Mrs Halliburton's Troubles,' 70.

Mivart, St George, 151.

'Modern' Essays (Myers), 172.

'Modern Painters,' 130, 132.

Molesworth, Rev. William Nassau. 'History of England, 1830-1873'; 'History of the Church of England,' 95.

'Molière,' by Mrs Oliphant, 74.

'Money,' 56.

'Monks of St Mark, The,' 62.

'Monograph on Charlotte Brontë,' 183.

Monthly Magazine, The, 42.

'Moonstone, The,' 69.

Moore, Thomas. The pioneer of the 'Celtic Renaissance'; 'Irish Melodies,' 33 ; 'Lalla Rookh'; 'Life of Byron,' 34.

Index

'More Leaves from the Journal of our Life in the Highlands,' 192.

'More Worlds than One,' 150.

Morison, James Cotter. Biographer of St Bernard of Clairvaux and Macaulay; 'The Service of Man,' 180.

Morley, John. Antagonist of 'Supernatural Christianity'; a gifted biographer and journalist; editor of *Morning Star*, *Literary Gazette*, *Fortnightly Review*, *Pall Mall Gazette*, and *Macmillan's Magazine*; editor of 'English Men of Letters Series'; 'Life of Burke'; influence, 181; lives of Voltaire, Rousseau, Diderot; 'Life of Cobden'; his essay 'On Compromise' probably the most exhaustive treatment of the question, 182.

Morley, John, and Macaulay, 93.

Morning Chronicle, The, 42.

Morning Star, 181.

Morris, Sir Lewis. Wrote 'Songs of Two Worlds'; 'Epic of Hades'; 'A Vision of Saints,' &c., 26.

Morris, William. Connection with Rossetti, 23; versatility of his genius; 'Dream of John Ball'; 'News from Nowhere,' 24; 'Defence of Guenevere'; 'Life and Death of Jason'; 'The Earthly Paradise,' 25.

Moulton, Mrs Chandler, 39.

Müller, Friedrich Max. Eminent Philologist; 'Lectures on the Science of Language'; 'Chips from a German Workshop,' 99; early religious systems, 100.

Mulock, Dinah. 'John Halifax,

Gentleman,' her best and most successful book, 72.

'Munera Pulveris,' 133.

Murchison, Sir Roderick Impey. Geologist; popularity of his 'Siluria,' 152.

Murray, Dr John, 155.

'My Beautiful Lady,' 23.

'My Cousin Nicholas,' 30.

Myers, Ernest, 173.

Myers, Frederick William Henry. 'Saint Paul'; his 'Classical' and 'Modern' critical essays full of delightful ideas; biography of Wordsworth, 172.

'Mythology of the Aryan Nations,' 100.

NANSEN, Dr, 186.

'Napoleon, A Short History of,' 105.

'National and Historical Ballads, Songs and Poems,' 34.

National Reformer, The, and 'The City of Dreadful Night,' 32.

'Natural History,' 153.

'Natural Religion,' 105.

'Naturalist's Voyage Round the World, A,' 155.

'Nelson Memorial, The,' 6.

'Nemesis of Faith,' 84.

'Never too Late to Mend,' 58.

'New Arabian Nights, The,' 60.

'Newcomes, The,' 45.

'New Magdalen, The,' 69.

Newman, Francis William. 'The Soul,' 'Theism,' 'Phases of Faith,' 170, 171.

Newman, John Henry. Early religious tendencies; 'My Battle with Liberalism,' 107; Matthew Arnold's description of Newman, 107-108; Tractarian movement;

217

Index

Index

Index

Index

Index

Index

Index

'Short History of the English People,' 97.

Shorthouse, Joseph Henry. 'John Inglesant'; 'Sir Perceval'; 'Little Schoolmaster Mark,' 64.

'Short Studies on Great Subjects,' 88.

Sidgwick, Henry. 'Principles of Political Economy'; 'Methods of Ethics'; a compromise; 'Elements of Politics,' 143.

'Silas Marner,' 50.

'Siluria,' 152.

'Sinai and Palestine,' 161.

'Sir Perceval,' 64.

'Sister Helen,' 24.

'Sketches by Boz,' 42.

'Sketch of the Life of Princess Alice,' 191.

Smith, Alexander, 31.

Smith, Goldwin. 'The Relations between England and America'; 'The Political Destiny of Canada,' 185.

Smith, H. Llewellyn, 144.

Smith, Sydney. 'The Ballot'; 'The Church Bills'; 'The Wit and Wisdom of Sydney Smith,' 187.

'Social Statics,' 145.

'Soldiers Three,' 40.

'Some Aspects of Robert Burns,' 60.

'Song of the Shirt,' 29.

'Song of the Sword,' 172.

'Song of the Western Men,' 38.

'Songs of Two Worlds,' 26.

'Song Tide and other Poems,' 39.

'Sonnets from the Portuguese,' 14.

'Sonnets on the War,' 31.

'Soul, The,' 170.

Southey, 5-7, 15.

'Spanish Gypsy,' 50.

Spedding, James. 'Letters and Life of Francis Bacon,' 184.

'Speeches and Addresses of the late Prince Consort,' 192.

Spencer, Herbert. The most characteristic philosopher of the century; 'On the Proper Sphere of Government'; *Nonconformist; Westminster Review;* 'Social Statics'; 'Principles of Psychology'; 'Education'; 'First Principles,' 145; 'Descriptive Sociology'; universality of his knowledge; his 'Study of Sociology' and 'Education' books which all who read must enjoy, 146.

'Spencer, Mr Herbert, and Mr G. H. Lewes: their Application of the Doctrine of Evolution to Thought,' 147.

'Spirit's Trials, The,' 84.

Spurgeon, Charles Haddon. Most distinguished Nonconformist minister of the period; 'John Ploughman's Talk,' 168.

Standard, The. Austin's connection with, 40.

Stanley, Arthur Penrhyn. 'Life of Dr Arnold'; 'Memorials of Canterbury'; 'Sinai and Palestine,' 161; 'Lectures on the Eastern Church'; 'Lectures on the Jewish Church'; leader of the Broad Church movement; proposed the suppression of the Athanasian creed in church services; his 'Life,' written by Dean Bradley, 162.

Stanley, H. M., 186.

Stanhope, Earl (Lord Mahon). 'History of the Reign of Queen

224

Index

Anne,' and 'History of England from 1713-1783,' 95.

'State in its Relations with the Church, The,' 106.

'Statesmen of the Commonwealth,' 179.

'Stein, Life and Times of,' 104.

Stephen, Leslie. A critic of remarkable learning; 'Hours in a Library'; 'History of English Thought in the Eighteenth Century,' 175; first editor of the *Dictionary of National Biography*, 176.

Stephen, Leslie, and Macaulay, 93.

Stevenson, Robert Louis. One of the most picturesque figures in literature; 'With a Donkey in the Cevennes,' 59; his plays; 'Beau Austin,' probably the greatest contribution to the drama of the era; 'Virginibus Puerisque'; 'Some Aspects of Robert Burns'; 'A Child's Garden of Verse'; 'Underwoods'; his place as a novelist; 'Treasure Island'; 'The New Arabian Nights'; 'The Master of Ballantrae'; 'Prince Otto'; 'St Ives'; 'Dr Jekyll and Mr Hyde,' 60; his admiration of 'The Egoist,' 61; his influence on the modern historical romance, 63.

Stewart, Balfour, 151.

'Stones of Venice,' 132.

'Story of My Heart, The,' 188.

'Stuart of Dunleath,' 72.

Stubbs, William. Librarian at Lambeth Palace; edited mediæval chronicles, 78; Regius Professor of History at Oxford;

'Select Charters'; 'Constitutional History'; profoundly scientific, but not dry-as-dust, 79.

'Student's Elements of Geology,' 152.

'Studies in Art and Poetry,' 171.

'Studies in Homer,' 106.

'Studies in Literature,' 173.

'Studies in Sensation and Event,' 37.

'Study of Sociology,' 146.

'Study of Spinoza,' 167.

'Strathmore,' 38.

Strauss, 49.

'Strayed Reveller, The,' 20.

Stretton, Mrs. Author of 'The Valley of a Hundred Fires,' 72.

'Structure and Distribution of Coral Reefs,' 155.

'Subjection of Women,' 139.

'Subscription no Bondage,' 164.

'Supernatural Religion,' 171.

'Supper at the Mill,' 29.

'Susan Hopley,' 71.

'Swallow Flights,' 39.

Swift, modern biographies of, 178.

Swinburne, Algernon Charles. Only comparable to Landor, 16; 'Ave atque Vale' an imperishable elegy; a great poet and a great prose writer, 17; connection with Rossetti, 24; admiration for Matthew Arnold, 17, and Emily Brontë, 48.

'Sybil,' 57.

'Sylvia's Lovers,' 71.

Symonds, John Addington. 'Renaissance in Italy,' 103; Cellini's 'Autobiography,' 104.

'TABLE TALK' (Rogers's), 183.

'Table Talk' (Southey's), 6.

'Tales of Ireland,' 66.

Index

Index

Index